Beyond Bin Laden

Global Terrorism Scenarios

Beyond Bin Laden
Global Terrorism Scenarios

Brig (Retd) Rahul K Bhonsle, SM

Vij Books India Pvt Ltd
New Delhi, India

Published by

Vij Books India Pvt Ltd
(Publishers, Distributors & Importers)
2/19, Ansari Road, Darya Ganj
New Delhi - 110002
Phones: 91-11-43596460, 91-11- 65449971
Fax: 91-11-47340674
e-mail : vijbooks@rediffmail.com
web: www.vijbooks.com

ISBN: 978-93-80177-99-1

CONTENTS

Chapter 1

"I welcome it [the killing of Osama Bin Laden] as a significant step forward and hope that it will deal a decisive blow to Al Qaeda and other terrorist groups. The international community and Pakistan in particular must work comprehensively to end the activities of all such groups who threaten civilized behaviour and kill innocent men, women and children."

India's Prime Minister Dr Manmohan Singh

Preview

This Chapter provides an introduction to the challenge of terrorism and a preview of the contents.

The linear world of counter terrorism witnessed a tsunami of sorts on 2 May 2011 with announcement by President Barack Obama that US Special Forces had succeeded in killing Osama Bin Laden, head of the Al Qaeda[1] and the most dreaded terrorist of modern times. The immediate result of this declaration was on the streets of New York and Washington where American people who had borne a sense of despondency ever since the flying passenger aircraft struck at the World Trade Towers on 9 September 2001, almost 10 years back were euphoric and slogans of, 'Long Live America,' rent the air There was also ebullience across much of the Western World as global leaders basked in the reflected glory of American success. The Indian government issued two statements unusual for the staid establishment in Raisina Hill, the seat of Indian state, one by the Prime Minister and another by the Home (internal security) Minister . Ironically rest of the World was muted and apart from Turkey none of the Islamic

---

[1] al Qaeda or Al Qaeda, both f orms have been used in the book randomly .

countries seemed to rejoice the death of Osama.

The Al Qaeda expectedly came out with a chilling message of revenge though a few days later while other terrorist groups as the   Taliban, first refused to accept the death and later followed up with threats against America and the West. These indicators denote that removal of Osama Bin Laden from the scene of global terror is likely to be in the most famous words of former United States Secretary of Defence Donald Rumsfield, "a unknown, unkown." Thus President Obama aptly remarked, "Qaeda remains dangerous, and we must be vigilant against attacks.   But we have put al Qaeda on a path to defeat, and we will not relent until the job is done". [2]

There was more pain to come as negative consequences of the killing seemed to be in direct proportion to the distance from the place of occurrence that is Abbottabad, a few metres away from Pakistan' s premier of ficer training academy and kilometers away from the national capital Islamabad. The operation carried out by United States Special Forces using stealth helicopters went unnoticed by Pakistan' s intelligence and military establishment. Osama's presence in the vicinity of a Cantonment also came as a surprise. The reputation and image of an intelligence agency and an army which was considered omnipotent was thus badly damaged as the shock of the event in their backyard waded into people's perception in the country.

Expectedly the reactions were rejectionist, reviling blatant violation of sovereignty by the United States. Shifting blame onAmerica was temporary reprieve for Pakistani agencies as political leaders as Nawaz Sharif bayed for the blood of military leaders and questioned the defence budget in the light of the country's penurious state. In a series of retributive raids which included the high security naval base PNS Mehran in Karachi the Taliban and Al Qaeda penetrated the security establishment causing heavy fatalities and further bruising the reputation of the militaryThere were other vectors, international and regional relations, internal political and militancy and

---

[2] The Whi te House. Office of the Pr ess Secretary. Remarks by the President on the W ay Forward in Afghanistan. June 22, 2011. http://www.whitehouse.gov/the-press-office/ 2011/06/22/remarks-president-way-forward-afghanistan

terrorism which were influenced by the event in Pakistan. On the larger plane thus the impact of death of Osama on global terrorism needs deeper analysis.

The main security paradigm across the globe in the post modern era is not war but counter terrorism. This is consuming billions of dollars, much of it from the coffers of some of the poorest economies and continuing to take many lives while spreading fear in millions. Osama was for long seen as the figurehead of global terrorism, a mascot for a small but radical group of Islamic youth across the World who were inspired by his ideology, image and use of mass terror to achieve the elusive Islamic Caliphate. The larger Muslim Ummah was skeptical even in his own land, Saudi Arabia, where Osama was a fugitive from law The Al Qaeda was also rejected in countries as Indonesia and India which have the largest Muslim population in the World.

But Osama successfully used modern media such as internet chat rooms and video streaming to spread his message of hate inspiring a small but, "critical mass," of youth who were willing to give up their way of life and turn to suicide terrorism which promised them martyrdom. He could do so without a dish antenna or an internet connection from his compound in Abbottabad for almost five years which is perhaps testimony to the stickiness of the Group's agenda of hate and the spread of its organisation.

Thus even as the Al Qaeda announced his successor expectedly Ayman al Zawahiri the nominal Second in Command almost a month later in mid June, envisaging the future trajectory of global terrorism and not just the deadly terrorist movement has become important, for applying Leon Trotsky's famous quote on war to terrorism, "you may not be interested in *terrorism*, but *terrorism* is interested in you".[3]

With that as the backdrop, this Book attempts to portray the likely scenarios in global terrorism, post Osama and counter terror strategies thereof with particular focus on the Al Qaeda. While there are close to 130

---

[3] Trotsky's famous quote read, "You may not be interested in war, but war is interested in you".

plus terrorist groups which have been banned by major global powers including the United States, Russia, European Union and India and many more who are spread across the World, almost all these organizations have a local and regional impact. It is al Qaeda alone which has attempted to spread terrorism globally, with the reach of its ideology and the spread of its network which influences all regions and countries of the   World from Australasia to Scandinavia and United States to Indonesia, thus providing a new benchmark. Al Qaeda's network of branches, affiliates and franchises enables it to influence a far larger population mass than any other terrorist group or a non-state or even some state actors. This influence is religious as well as cultural a way of life it portrays as an alternative to modernity which can attract deviants, aggrieved and even those are seeking violent adventure.

Materially the al Qaeda provides money , a base for training and sanctuary for hiding to disparate groups as the Islamic Mujahideen of Uzbekistan (IMU) or prospective lone ranger terrorists from Germany. Its ability to operate with a miniscule support base from the Muslim Ummah to feed the devilish cycle of violence provides a model for other groups to emulate. By skillfully exploiting the narrative more than the ideologythat of hatred of the United States, a sense of persecution in the Muslim community and artificial schisms between Islam and theWest, Bin Laden was successful in projecting terror particularly in South and   West Asia as well as North Africa while threatening parts of Europe andAmerica. Thus in many ways the trajectory of the al Qaeda will determine the pathway of global terrorism in the years ahead.

The overall threat from terrorism will be evident from an empirical survey of fatalities globally as well as in one of the most affected regions South Asia as shown inTable 1 and 2 below respectively Each table should be examined independently as global statistics in   Table 1 do not include fatalities in insurgency incidents whileTable 2 SouthAsia includes the latter hence there is a variation in the figures. There have been almost 90,000 deaths due to terror in the past from 2005 to 2009 globally which is almost the same number in South Asia from 2005 to June 201 1 where deaths in insurgency are also included. These numbers underline gravity of the challenge of terrorism. More over the trend remains non linear going up in 2006 and

4

2007 while coming down in 2008 and 2009, thereby indicating concerted action by concerned global citizens.

Terrorism Global Statistics						
	2005	**2006**	**2007**	**2008**	**2009**	**Total**
Terrorist Attacks	11,023	14,443	14,435	11,725	10,999	62,625
Fatalities	14,482	20,515	22,736	15,727	14,971	88,431

Table 1[4]

South Asia Fatalities : 2 005-2011*				
Year	**Civilians**	**SFs**	**Terrorists**	**Total**
2005	1987	920	3301	6208
2006	2803	1725	4509	9037
2007	3128	1503	6126	10757
2008	3677	2314	14742	20733
2009	14197	2738	12703	29638
2010	2571	844	6016	9431
2011 [Upto July 12]	1575	585	1824	3984
Total*	**29938**	**10629**	**49221**	**89788**

Table 2[5]

---

[4] US Department of State. Country R eports on Terrorism 2009. A ugust 2010. Available at http://www.state.gov/documents/organization/141114.pdf

[5] South Asia Terrorism Portal. Figures are compiled from news reports and are provisional as per the S ATP. Available at ht tp://www.satp.org/satporgtp/southasia/datasheets/Fatalities.html accessed on 16 July 2011.

If 9/11 is identified as a milestone of global terrorism, than the period in which the World has been held in the spell of this traditional mode of conflict will soon exceed the combined span of the First [1914-1919] as well as the Second World Wars [1939-1945]. There are at present 104 organisations across the globe on the United Nations sanctions list for links to the Al Qaeda. In addition there are many more who remain below the horizon. Thus the spatial expanse and reach of terrorism is spread unlike the World wars across all Continents.

But terrorism is not just about numbers. The key vectors of terrorism are ideology and narrative, mass and core support and organization for realization of goals. Ironically while the base supporting terrorism can be low so long as the narrative can attract sufficient followers, it will continue to thrive. For instance a large majority of Muslims across the World do not subscribe to Al Qaeda ideology of violent extremism or even establishment of an Islamic Caliphate; however there is sympathy for the group's narrative of persecution of Islam and an unjust international order dominated by the United States and West. The al Qaeda has been able to mobilize support of sufficient numbers by this narrative witness the muted response to killing of Osama in the Islamic world. At the same time by its ideology it has lured a small core of radical youth who are willing to be martyrs to the cause.

The organizational factors supporting terrorism include leadership, groups to include branches and affiliates, information, financial and arms support networks, training infrastructure and media. These are also regarded by some as demand and supply factors of terror, ideology and grievances creating demand while organization providing the supply. The spread of terrorism in space and time necessitates closure of this vile chapter in the history of human violence as unlike war it impacts the every day life of millions of innocent citizens across the globe.

There are thus five reasons why defeating the Al Qaeda is important in the years ahead. Firstly, it is the only non state actor which has global influence and a transnational presence across Asia and Africa. Secondly, the narrative of persecution by the West attracts a large mass of population while the ideology of the Caliphate through terror a core group of youth who are willing to carry out terrorist attacks resulting in mass casualties. Thirdly, the al Qaeda is challenging the state system, its defeat will signal the triumph of the S tate over the non-state. Fourthly , its destruction will have a domino effect on other groups who can be marginalized relatively easily. Fifthly, and perhaps most importantly the al Qaeda is also aspiring to acquire nuclear, biological and chemical capability which may have catastrophic results in case the group succeeds.

While many perspectives can be used to study terrorism, this Book attempts to employ how terrorism ends as the central conceptual framework. The basic premise is that if we know the manner in which terror ends, charting a course towards the same will be that much easier.

A number of studies have been carried out to examine how terrorism ends. Two seminal works, one by the premier American think tank, Rand Corporation, "*How ter rorist gr oups end: lessons for countering Al Qa'ida*", and another byAudrey Kurth Cronin, an internationally renowned terrorism expert "*How Terrorism Ends: Understanding the Decline and Demise of T errorist Campaigns ,*" have been taken as a benchmark and the end of trajectory of al Qaeda and current wave of terror measured against the same by using the scenario building technique.

A detailed review of these studies is given out in the succeeding Chapter entitled, "How will Al Qaeda end? Chapter 3 covers Operation Neptune Spear, the US Special Forces operation that led to the assassination of Osama Bin Laden. Chapter 4, "Al Qaeda Beyond Bin Laden," discusses the background of Bin Laden and Al Qaeda, its current profile and possible future trajectory. Chapter 5 examines the fall out of Bin Laden' s death in South Asia. In Chapter 6 a survey of how India successfully evaded the threat of the Al Qaeda has been analysed. In Chapter 7, four possible scenarios of al Qaeda and global terrorism have been discussed while the final Chapter examines strategies to achieve the ideal scenario for containing global terrorism with specific reference to SouthAsia.

Chapter 2

How Al Qaeda Will End?

This chapter examines various studies on ending terrorism and their application to the Al Qaeda, options for containing state support to terrorism and conditions required to be created for effective implementation of strategies discussed.

"The world is safer. It is a better place because of the death of Osama bin Laden," declared President Barack Obama on 2 May 2011 announcing the success of United S tates Seal operation in Abbottabad Pakistan. Understandably there was euphoria across the United States and particularly in New York and Washington where crowds celebrated throughout the night. The victim's families felt that justice had been done. Mike Low father of Sara a flight attendant of the hijacked plane that crashed into the World Trade Centre North Tower said, "For my family and me, it' s good, it' s desirable, it's right. It certainly brings an ending to a major quest for all of us."

An Al Qaeda commentator calling himself asAssad al-Jihad however wrote online, "Woe to his enemies. By God, we will avenge the killing of the Sheik of Islam. Those who wish that jihad has ended or weakened, I tell them: Let us wait a little bit." United S tates Central Intelligence Agency (CIA) Director Leon Panetta thus rightly commented, "Bin Laden is dead. Al-Qaida is not."

Understanding how al Qaeda will end will naturally entail examining how terrorism ends? As terrorism is a socio political phenomenon a perspective from the political or strategic and social sciences is necessary to understand the underlying motivations of terrorist groups. A common belief is that groups resort to terrorism only when they believe that gains from the same outweigh costs as well as benefits from alternate forms of protest. Another view is that when states find other forms of coercion or cooperation does not facilitate achievement of national objectives or protection of national interest they may sponsor terrorist groups to achieve the same. The, "strategic model," highlights political utility of terrorism. The, "natural systems model" examines terrorism from a social gains perspective of how individuals gain from participation in a social group or enterprise providing them a sense of empowerment. [2] As we see subsequently both paradigms are relevant to evolve strategies for ending terror.

Terrorism has to address the roots of many problems. One is the pathological hatred of individuals who take a position against a particular ideology or community such as Bin Laden against America or LTTE leader Prabhakaran against the Sinhala. Gradually this hatred may expand beyond the leader to the whole community creating divides which become unbreachable if not addressed with alacrity . These may then transmutate beyond communities to governments and nation states by when the challenge will become even worse and countering it will necessitate a transnational if not global effort. Global terrorist groups as the Al Qaeda then take over such movements to give it a colour of clash of civilisations, or typify with the medieval crusades. This is perhaps the ultimate socio political form that terrorism has attained and thus defeating it may require a far more comprehensive strategy than adapted so far.

There have been a number of studies on how terrorism ends, here two principal and a number of subsidiary ones are examined. The two main ones are by Rand Corporation published in 2008 and the second by Dr Audrey Kurth Cronin a professor at the US National War College entitled, "How Terrorism Ends," published in 2009. The subsidiary works include

---

[1] Max Abrahms. What Terrorists Really Want: Terrorist Motives and Counterterrorism Strategy International Security 2008 32:4, 78-105

[2] Max Abrahms. What Terrorists Really Want: Terrorist Motives and Counterterrorism Strategy International Security 2008 32:4, 78-105

Dipak Gupta, a professor in San Diego S   tate University, California, *"Understanding Terrorism and Political V iolence,"* (2008) and the author's own previous work, " *Countering Transnational Terrorism."* (2011). The latter examines how state sponsorship to terror can be terminated.

Most theoretical models developed on end of terrorism since 1968 seems to suggest that terrorism ends primarily due to effective local and police actions by intelligence agencies or because they join the political process abandoning violent means to come to power . [3] Similarly state support to terrorism will end when there is a congruence of interests between contending nations who see a common threat emerging from a group or leader that one state fostered willingly or unwillingly against the other . The example of cooperation between India and Sri Lanka against the Liberation of Tamil Tigers (LTTE) and India and Bangladesh to decapacitate a number of leaders of groups operating from that country in India's North Eastern region seem to confirm this assertion.[4] A detailed survey is carried out in the succeeding paragraphs.

The Study by Seth G Jones and Martin Libicki for the Rand Corporation in 2008 has identified five major ways and other minor causes due to which terrorist groups end to include, "policing, military force, splintering, politics, or victory," with the addendums of, "providing economic aid to countries dealing with terrorism, imposing economic sanctions on states that harbour terrorist groups, dissuading groups by hardening targets, improving intelligence, or engaging in diplomacy". Practically terrorism ends by application of a combination of all these factors but the application of each strategy has to prioritise on these.[5]

The Rand Study has analysed terrorist groups that existed worldwide between 1968 and 2006. The study was based on data of terrorist groups

---

[3] Seth G. Jones, Martin C. Libicki,*How terrorist groups end: lessons for countering Al Qa'ida* Rand Santa Monica. 2008

[4] Rahul K Bhonsle, *Countering Transnational Terrorism,* New Delhi. Vij Books India Pvt Ltd, 2011. pp 107-109.

[5] Seth G. Jones, Martin C. Libicki,*How terrorist groups end : lessons for countering Al Qa'ida* Rand Santa Monica. 2008

between 1968 and 2006 from Rand and the Memorial Institute for the Prevention of Terrorism incident data base. The various factors used to analyse the data were how issues such as the type of regime, size, ideology and goals of groups and economic conditions facilitated their survival. The Study identified that of the 648 groups active between 1968 and 2006, 268 ended during the same period, 136 groups splintered, and 244 continued to be active. Those that ended were mainly due to penetration and elimination by local police and intelligence agencies (40 percent) or peaceful political accommodation with the government (43 percent). 10 percent groups surveyed achieved their political goals while in 7 percent of the cases they were militarily defeated. [6]

Dr Audrey Kurth Cronin's study of how terrorism ends includes terrorist groups for the past two centuries including the African National Congress, Liberation of Tamil Tigers Ealam (LTTE) and Real Irish Republican Army. Cronin has highlighted six ways terrorism campaigns end: decapitation; negotiation; success; failure; repression; and reorientation.

Gupta seems to suggest that terrorism could have three endings, victory and formation of a legitimate government, transformation into a criminal organisation and termination of the movement. Termination of the movement can occur due to military defeat, ideological irrelevance, joining the political system or a negotiated end to violence[7]. There are thus apparent congruities in the three studies as is indicated in Table 1 opposite.

---

[6] Seth G. Jones, Martin C. Libicki, *How terrorist groups end : lessons for countering Al Qa'ida* Rand Santa Monica. 2008

[7] Dipak K Gupta, *Understanding Terrorism and Political Violence,* Routledge. Oxon. 2008. P 98 -100

How Terrorism Ends?

Cronin Study	Rand Study	Dipak Gupta's Study
Decapitation; negotiation; success; failure; repression; and reorientation	Five major ways "policing, military force, splintering, politics, or victory." Common themes will also include dissuasion of groups by hardening targets and improving intelligence which will support these strategies. [8]	Irrelevance of political goals due to changed political reality, loss of support base, exhaustion, military defeat, leader decapacitation when applied to a small group, negotiated settlement and success.

Table 1

To summarise these studies seem to suggest five main ways in which terrorism could end, decapacitation, negotiations after a group has been sufficiently prepared either through decimation of cadres, suturing support base or change in political goals, military defeat through a combination of policing, intelligence and armed action, abject failure and finally success. Practically, though terrorism is seen to fail due to an adroit combination of these factors. A State will have to thus prioritise the strategy to be applied at various stages of a counter terror campaign. [9] What is also to be noted is that terrorism can achieve success, thus there is all the more reason to examine this phenomenon more closely with reference to the Al Qaeda, for victory of this movement will imply reordering of the existing universal value systems as well.

---

[8] Seth G. Jones, Martin C. Libicki.*How terrorist groups end : lessons for countering Al Qa'ida* Rand Santa Monica, 2008

[9] Seth G. Jones, Martin C. Libicki.*How terrorist groups end : lessons for countering Al Qa'ida* Rand Santa Monica, 2008

Examining Means to EndTerror

Decapacitation

Taking decapacitation first given the proximity of Bin Laden' death. Some as Cronin include decapacitation of leaders as a separate strategy but Jones and Libicki consider this as a part of the policing or military strategy   . [10] Decapitation – killing or arrest of a leader has a number of connotations to include the impact on the or ganisation, its capability , the ethical issues highlighted by some even in the killing of Osama Bin Laden and the overall psychological impact. This strategy has these and other limitations particularly the mass base that an ideology or a cause may have thus she says, "Human nature is such that, when a cause is well established and has built up a significant following, killing its mouthpiece and organizer will not end its viability"[11]

For Al Qaeda Cronin portends that elimination of the leaders per se may not lead to demise of the group nor crushing it by force or negotiations is likely to achieve results. On the other hand implosion or diminishing popular support provides better possibilities while the most worrisome is that of expanding towards full scale insurgency at least in parts where it is dominant and there is anarchy due to absence of the state.   [12]

The other forms of decapacitation include arrest of the leader or converting him from violence to political action to achieve his goalsArrest of a leader may reduce the effectiveness of an organisation; some salient examples quoted by Cronin include that ofAbimael Guzman's arrest and its impact on the Shining Path in Peru or Abdullah Ocalan and the Kurdistan Worker's Party.

---

[10] Seth G. Jones, Martin C. Libicki.   *How terrorist groups end : lessons for countering Al Qa'ida.* Rand Santa Monica. 2008 Terrorist Campaigns . Princeton, NJ: PrincetonUnivPress, 2009. P 34.

[11] A udrey Kurth Cronin, *How Terrorism Ends: Understanding the Decl ine and Demise of Terrorist Campaigns* . Princeton, NJ: Princeton Univ . Press, 2009. P 34 .

[12] Audrey Kurth Cronin, *How Terrorism Ends: Understanding the Decine and Demise of Terrorist Campaigns* . Princeton, NJ: Princeton Univ .Press, 2009. P 191.

This may not imply success in all cases, for instance in Russia, the Foreign Ministry compared the killing of Bin Laden to that of Shamil Basayev the Chechnya Terrorist leader. However just as Basayev' s death has not seen the end of terror in North Caucasus that of Bin Laden is not likely to across the globe.

Negotiations

When a large population supports terrorists, negotiated settlement will provide the only solution a lesson well understood by democracies but may be frequently ignored by authoritarian states. In evaluating negotiations as a counter terrorism strategy, Cronin notes that there are various motives for democracies to negotiate to include the need to end violence, split the group, and undermine its support base and also to develop greater intelligence about its activities. For negotiations that can lead to a lasting conclusion there is a need for a strong leadership with a sound purpose and possibly a third party for mediation though she concedes that negotiation alone may not yield expected results. [13]

Terrorist groups are human organisms and thus undergo a variety of transformations some of which can be triggered by intelligence agencies thereby rendering them more amenable for neutralisation. These transformations can be termed variously as, "cross pollination (shift of leaders or individual fighters from one group to another), fertilization (fusion of groups producing new ones), hybridization (combinations to achieve specific aims and objectives) and centrifugalism (formation of new groups by dissenting leaders)".[14]

Engineering split between the pragmatists vis a vis the radical ideologues who are likely to reject negotiations is an essential facet of use of this technique. When the radicals are split they have the option of either going in for a compromise or pursue their goals with a smaller organisation and

---

[13] Audrey Kurth Cronin, *How Terrorism Ends: Understanding the Decline and Demise of Terrorist Campaigns* . Princeton, NJ: Princeton Univ .Press, 2009. P 34 .

[14] Rahul K Bhonsle. *Countering Transnational Terrorism,* New Delhi. Vij Books India Pvt Ltd, 2011. P 40.

support base. The example of Nepal again would be instructive. Nepal's Maoists have three main streams, the Prachanda and the Bhattarai factions led by Chairman Dahal and Deputy Chairman Baburam Bhattarai are moderates while the one led by Mohan Vaidya is radical. While all three came together to sign the Comprehensive Peace Agreement in 2006, Mohan Vaidya faction possibly did so with the hope of carrying the flag of revolution once an opportunity so presented. The group is therefore seen as an outlier and may or may not join the final political arrangement as per indications in June 2011. At the same time by working on moderate factions, the insurgency which raged in the country in the late 1990's taking over 13,000 lives has given way to political reconciliation. However as per Cronin where violence is the rational for the very existence of a group, it is unlikely to relent and will avoid participation in negotiations.

In the case of groups achieving their objectives through negotiations the narrower the goals the easier it was to accommodate them and achieve success through parleys.[15] Some terrorist groups are amenable to a political solution. Thus the Irish Republican Army (IRA) and Palestine Liberation Organization (PLO) also considered political dialogue as the base for a solution. Taking the case of Al Qaeda, the organisation or movement has expansive goals therefore it is unlikely that it can be accommodated unless the group changes its goals and restricts its objectives. Similarly for accommodation of the Taliban goals of the oganisation have to be harmonized with that of the government of Afghanistan. This may result in an agreement to share power sharing provided the rebels feel that the arrangement is inclusive. This has been the case in Nepal where the Communist Party of Nepal (Maoist) which is now known as the Unified CPN M signed a Comprehensive Peace Agreement with other political parties to shed violence in 2006 and came to power in elections though the shift from the gun to the ballot is yet a work in progress.

Military Force

Military remains a key instrument against large terrorist groups holding vast

---

[15] Seth G. Jones, Martin C. Libicki. *How terrorist groups end : lessons for countering Al Qa'ida*. Rand Santa Monica. 2008

territory and with an expansive organisation. Cronin is very much against strategy of repression or use of military force by the state as it seems to lead to what she calls, "a pyrrhic victory. If the ideas that are the source of popular mobilization persist, repression will be temporary , even counterproductive." [16]

There are other problems in a strategy purely based on repression as the Sri Lankan government seems to have realised now where it has become the subject of intense scrutiny over mass human rights violations with a United Nations nominated Experts Panel report indicting the government. This has also weakened the response that it can offer and held the government hostage to political bargaining thereby reducing its overall strategic quotient. In this context Cronins observation may also be relevant. "The core of the relationship is between states and communities that are competing over the capacity to mobilize support, and it is success or failure in that dimension which ultimately determines whether or not repression ends terrorism" [17]

The Sri Lankan government has been able to successfully mobilise support of the majority Sinhala community for the end of the war with the LTTE thereby President Mahinda Rajapaksa was able to win another term, yet he has very limited support from the Tamils the other protagonists in the ethnic dyad. This partial support has raised issues of legitimacy of the repression by the regime as well as contribution to a final solution which remains elusive even two years after end of the violent conflict in May 2009.

Other Endings

A group can fail due to loss of support, alienation of its support base, inability to transcend the ideology or cause to the next generation, ideological differences, lack of interest or as is evident in many of cases in India sheer

---

[16] Audrey Kurth Cronin, *How Terrorism Ends: Understanding the Decline and Demise of Terrorist Campaigns,* Princeton, NJ: Princeton Univ .Press, 2009. P 141.

[17] Audrey Kurth Cronin, *How Terrorism Ends: Understanding the Decline and Demise of Terrorist Campaigns,* Princeton, NJ: Princeton Univ .Press, 2009. P 145.

exhaustion. Hard core terrorism may divest into other forms including criminal terror at one end to an insurgency and a civil war on the other [18] Left Wing terrorism seems to be more popular in higher income countries so also is nationalism however religious inspiration was seen to be more prevalent in the developing an under developed world. Cronin seems to indicate that ethnic separatist campaigns are harder to end than politically based ones.

The Rand study concludes that religious groups did not achieve their aim during the period studied, though there were fewer organisations then who had that motivation than those possibly operating now globally with religious extremism having become the main ideological vector for terrorism.[19] Never the less this should give relief to those planning counter Al Qaeda and Taliban strategies despite the gloomy picture emerging from the Af Pak region over the past few years.

Success

Success through terrorism can be defined as achievement of political or strategic goals of an organisation for which the tools of terror have been employed. [20] Success has not been as elusive for large groups as is commonly believed. African National Congress (ANC) leader , Nelson Mandela imprisoned for 26 years till 1990 had remarked in his trial in 1964, "without violence there would be no way open to the African people to succeed in their struggle against the principle of white supremacyAll lawful modes of expressing opposition to this principle had been closed by legislation, and we were placed in a position in which we had either to accept a permanent state of inferiority , or to defy the Government." The ANC's last act of terror was in 1989 and in 1990 it joined the political mainstream to come to power later. Other examples of success of terrorism are that of , the FLN against the French inAlgeria (1954–1962) and the Igun and Lohamei Herut

[18] Audrey Kurth Cronin, *How Terrorism Ends: Understanding the Decline and Demise of Terrorist Campaigns* . Princeton, NJ: PrincetonUniv .Press, 2009. P 149.

[19] Seth G. Jones, Martin C. Libicki. *How terrorist groups end : lessons for countering Al Qa'ida.* Rand Santa Monica. 2008

[20] Audrey Kurth Cronin, *How Terrorism Ends: Understanding the Decl ine and Demise of Terrorist Campaigns* . Princeton, NJ: Princeton Univ .Press, 2009. P 34 .

Israel (Lehi) against the British during the Palestine Mandate (1937–1948).[21]

Terrorist acts can create two ef fects, resentment against an organisation's political agenda due to mass scale of violence perpetrated or an increase in membership due to the act by enhancing morale and providing a sense of success. The African National Congress for instance achieved the policy goals, "despite the use of violence against innocent civilians [rather] than because of it."

Similarly large groups over 10,000 were normally victorious vis a vis smaller ones at least 25 percent of the time while those below 1000 seldom achieved victory.[22] This factor may denote that the Al Qaeda and Taliban both having a large profile the latter expectedly as per NATO sources having over 25,000 fighters have a good chance for success if they persevere. This may be one of the reasons why despite many overtures the Taliban are nowhere inking an agreement with the government. A lesson that possibly emerges is that counter terrorist policy planners should aim at fractionalising the larger groups into smaller entities who can then be negotiated into the main stream.

In Cronin's final analysis it is the support base that a group has that will determine the course it takes, if that dwindles the group will perish but if the same expands the group may transcend to higher forms from terrorism to insurgency and civil war .[23] A broad overview of the progression of the LTTE which at one stage could muster support globally including many of states which had sizeable Tamil diaspora abroad and its demise which was an indirect function of squeezing of the support base by imposing sanctions, neutralising financial and arms network and interception of routes of supply Cutting off the supply chain created conditions for launching a successful military campaign against it.

[21] Seth G. Jones, Martin C. Libicki. *How terrorist groups end : lessons for countering Al Qa'ida.* Rand Santa Monica. 2008

[22] Seth G. Jones, Martin C. Libicki. *How terrorist groups end : lessons for countering Al Qa'ida.* Rand Santa Monica. 2008

[23] Audrey Kurth Cronin, *How Terrorism Ends: Understanding the Decline and Demise of Terrorist Campaigns* . Princeton, NJ: Princeton Univ . Press, 2009. P 166.

Ending AlQaeda?

For the Al Qaeda, Cronin, feels that negotiation, failure and reorientation are realistic scenarios. But the challenge remains that of negotiation with whom? Failure by what means and reorientation towards what direction, these are some of the questions which remain unanswered. Cronin agrees that it may not be realistic to negotiate with the   Al Qaeda Central with Ayman al Zawahiri at the head, but there is a possibility of negotiating with branches and affiliates of this conglomerate. However ethical considerations may also impinge on reaching such agreements for this would be seen by many and particularly the victims of terror perpetrated by the guerrillas as dishonourable.

Yet states are known to have made such compromises. Recently in India the United Liberation Front ofAssam's ChairmanArabinda Rajakhowa was assured amnesty by the government if he forsakes violence even though victims of violence in the State of Assam protested. Rajakhowa undertook a special drive to appease them by apologizing for violence by the group and at present negotiations with the government are still ongoing.

Targeting Al Qaeda's credibility and narrative thereby reducing the appeal that it reflects in a certain section of the Islamic community globally is possible. Cronin also seems to suggest directing al Qaeda towards insurgency and crime as another possibility to finally defeat it. Though for manifestation into an insurgency mass support is necessary which the outfit may succeed in gaining locally and regionally rather than globally. One of Cronin's assertions may be proving correct at least in the short term that decapacitation of Bin Laden will not see the end of the group as Zawahiri has taken over in what could be seen as a reasonably smooth transition, being portrayed by the guerrillas as through consensus of the leadership spread across Asia and North Africa. That this could take place within a month and a half of Bin Laden's demise indicates that the network is working.

The Al Qaeda's selection of tar gets may also determine the support that it would have in the days ahead. In case the group continues to target civilians vis a vis security forces it is likely to lose the support base, for

20

killing of innocents in many ways does not explain the goals of the organisation to the population. [24] Al Qaeda's strategic leadership is well aware of these nuances. Thus major terrorist attacks outside the regional ambit are invariably approved by the central authority and when these are conducted without the same as by the Al Qaeda in Iraq under Zaraqawi did in Jordan in November 2005, the leader is chastised openlyThus the role of the strategic leadership in designating the type of terrorist attacks is the focus of the central leadership due to its correlation with effect.

Bin Laden and Zawahiri are the symbols of defiance of America and thus have been appealing to the community from where they draw popular support. They have not just manipulated the 9/11 attacks but evaded capture by the Americans in Tora Bora immediately after Operation Enduring Freedom swept Afghanistan and remained at lar ge for almost a decade which created an aura around them. Their ability to inspire their own ilk, the Taliban in Afghanistan as well as Pakistan and groups as the Lashkar e Taiyyaba to carry out attacks across the World including London, Madrid, Bali and Mumbai has created a legend of sorts. Puncturing this legend is important. While part of this has been achieved, targeting of Zawahiri may prove the turning point, for this would splinter theAl Qaeda effectively into various branches and affiliates. Whosoever emerges a leader to succeed Zawahiri does not have the cultivated image of a global terrorist, "hero," that the present Al Qaeda leader had along with Bin Laden. Recreating the myth will take time, a gap enough for the counter terrorist campaign to destroy the guerrillas across the board.

The danger of proliferation of nuclear terror is considered high given that nuclear technology has been available widely for over six decades. Some states are seen as potential threats for proliferation such as North Korea which may expand into the non state dimension. Al Qaeda is determined to obtain nuclear weapons and this desire is not restricted to Bin Laden but has been expressed by others in the group. The possibility of the group now determining acquisition of nuclear or a radiological weapon to

---

[24] Seth G. Jones, Martin C. Libicki. *How terrorist groups end : lessons for countering Al Qa'ida.* Rand Santa Monica. 2008

cause mass destruction thereby avenge the death of Bin Laden thus remains high.

Ending State Sponsorship of Terror

State Support to Terrorism	**Rand Study** - Economic aid, sanctions and diplomacy.[25]
	Author's Study - Inter State cooperation, diplomacy, economic a nd t rade s anctions, military and development aid and assistance, war. [26]

Table 2

The transformation of terrorism from a tactical tool of insurgents in the 1970's to state sponsorship tacit or even overt is one of the significant phenomenon of the post modern era. The support by states could also be passive due to poor governance thereby providing free space for terrorist groups to operate such as in the tribal areas of Pakistan in the 2008-09 and persisting even after launch of counter terrorist operations by the countrys' military. There can also be significant backlash from this strategy where the hand that feeds can also become the victim of terror . [27]

Employment of terrorism by States as a policy happens when national decision making is restricted to a narrow elite say a militaryr an authoritarian regime. For instance referring to the support of terrorism by the Pakistan state well known columnist Fareed Zakaria writes, "Until the Pakistani military truly takes on a more holistic view of the countrys' national interests — one that sees economic development, not strategic gamesmanship against Afghanistan and India, as the key to Pakistan' s security — terrorists will continue to find Pakistan an ideal place to go shopping".[28]

---

[25] Seth G. Jones, Martin C. Libicki. *How terrorist groups end : lessons for countering Al Qa'ida*. Rand Santa Monica. 2008

[26] Rahul K Bhonsle, *Countering Transnational Terrorism*. New Delhi. Vij Books. 2011.

[27] Rahul K Bhonsle, *Countering Transnational Terrorism*. New Delhi. Vij Books. 2011. P.74

[28] Rahul K Bhonsle, *Countering Transnational Terrorism*. New Delhi. Vij Books. 2011. P. 86.

States can also try to differentiate between groups which are harmful and those that can by controlled to perpetuate their strategy externally   . Manipulation of groups to support the ideology from time to time, formation and encouragement of new groups to suit variation in aims and strategy by states is also common. For instance the ISI first supported groups such as the Jammu and Kashmir Liberation Front (JKLF) which pursued independence in Kashmir , then turned their attention to J & K Hizbul Mujahideen or HM which was inclined towards Pakistan. When this too did not fit the ISI aims, the attention the Lashkar e   Taiyyaba and the Jaish e Mohammad were created which comprised of mainly Pakistani youth from the improvished province of South Punjab to foster militancy in Jammu and Kashmir. [29]

State leaders can also praise terrorist groups obliquely In what is seen as a reference to support of Nicaraguan contra rebels, Ronald Reagan former President of the United States said in 1986, "Freedom Fighters do not need to terrorise a population into submission. Freedom fighters target the military forces and organized instruments of repression keeping dictatorial regimes in power. Freedom fighters struggle to liberate their citizens from oppression and to establish a form of government that reflects the will of the people". Reagan's critics also accuse him sanctioning raising the Afghan Mujahideen to fight the Soviet Union during the Cold War, a monster that has morphed into amongst others the Al Qaeda.[30]

Under the circumstances the options that would have to be exercised for ending a States support to terrorism could be varied and would range from a conventional war to diplomacy with actions at lower scales of intensity as localised limited wars, border wars or shooting wars employed with the aim of deterrence. Economic sanctions and trade embargoes are also evident tools in this dynamic.[31] Employment of military and development aid is another tool though its ef fectiveness remains suspect. As per observations by Dr Christine Fair for instance US military and development assistance to Pakistan

---

[29] Rahul K Bhonsle, *Countering Transnational Terrorism*. New Delhi. Vij Books India. 2011. P.40.

[30] Scott Shane, Warfare with Words. *Indian Express* New Delhi. 7 April 2010. p 11.

[31] Rahul K Bhonsle, *Countering Transnational Terrorism*. New Delhi. Vij Books India. 2011. P 161.

is also seen by locals as a strategic tool to foster American interests rather than to assist in Pakistan's security and development.This partially explains continued anti US sentiment despite heavy pouring of aid and assistance to Islamabad.[32] Despite these apprehensions engagement of foreign governments in a cooperative venture is essential.

The fruits of inter state cooperation have been borne by the success from 2008 to 201 1 in South Asia with the comprehensive defeat of the LTTE. This was mainly due to the military ef fort of the Sri Lankan government despite its warts but also due to support ironically by India, China and Pakistan, three mutually adversarial states. Similarly the India Bangladesh cooperation after theAwami League government came to power in Dhaka in December 2008 but which was nurtured during two years of Caretaker Administration supported by the Bangladesh military has resulted in a number of top ranking terrorist groups leaders from Indian North Eastern states ofAssam, Manipur andTripura either joining the process of negotiations or being legally brought to book.

Creating Conditions for Ending Terrorism

Terrorism is a manifestation of ideological and environmental conditions for growth of radical ideologies and violent groups in a society . The latter replicate what is commonly known as, ungoverned spaces also referred to in extreme cases as failed states. Restoration of order is a primary function to create conditions to end terrorism.This will include security governance and development responses. Deterrence by enhancing safety and security by hardening possible targets and organising forces for pre-emptive action based on information and intelligence would be the first function of the state under this paradigm.

Creating cultural conditions for ending support to terror by counter and deradicalisation of society is equally important. Radicalisation has been defined in many forms, but one that could be employed in context is, "the

---

[32] C. Christine F air. Try to see i t my way. http://afpak.foreignpolicy.com/posts/2011/05/24/ try_to_see_it_my_way

process by which individuals—usually young people—are introduced to an overtly ideological message and belief system that encourages movement from moderate, mainstream beliefs towards extreme views."[33] Some writers have also termed the overall support garnered by the al Qaeda as, "neo jihadism," which amongst other characteristics includes manipulation of benign versions of religious scriptures and also most significantly revenge as one of the key precepts. [34]

Conversely deradicalisation should motivate individuals and groups to reverse the path to extremism. This will defuse the ideology and narrative pandered by terrorist groups as the al Qaeda who project radicalism. These measures would encompass political, social, economic, legal and structural interventions and are easier to implement in pluralist societies.[35] The most effective programme will however remain that initiated by community and religious leaders from the population base of the terrorists.

In this context the Indian programme for deradicalisation is largely led by the Islamic community. Thus on 31 May 2008 clerics from one of the most famous and accepted Islamic religious school, the Deoband issued a fatwa declaring terrorism and violence as un-Islamic. [36] This was one in a series of such pronouncements by the organisation and has a seminal impact on the community. Ironically the Taliban claim to be Deobandis though the ideology has been hijacked over the years with growth of an extremist form in Pakistan. Counter and deradicalisation will therefore be an important programme to create conditions to end terrorism.

---

[33] Pete Lentini. The Transference of Neojihadism: Towards a Process Theory of Transnational Radicalisation. http://arts.monash.edu.au/politics/terror-research/proceedings/gtrec-proceedings-2009-01-pete-lentini.pdf

[34] Pete Lentini. The Transference of Neojihadism: Towards a Process Theory of Transnational Radicalisation. http://arts.monash.edu.au/politics/terror-research/proceedings/gtrec-proceedings-2009-01-pete-lentini.pdf

[35] Rahul K Bhonsle, *Countering Transnational Terrorism*. New Delhi. Vij Books India. 2011. P 175

[36] Kamala Kanta Dash. The Fatwa against Terrorism: Indian Deobandis Renounce Violence but Policing Remains Unchanged. http://monash.academia.edu/KamalaKantaDash/Papers197756The_Fatwa_Against_Terrorism_Indian_Deobandis_Renounce_Violence_but_Policing_ Remains_Unchanged

Conclusion

A study of how terrorism ends will not be conclusive without highlighting the necessity for states to persevere single-mindedly with the objective of defeating it, for this form challenges is an existential threat to the Westphalian state system. A group may fail due to a variety of reasons but a state cannot wait for a group to fail and has to carefully push it towards failure.   As Audrey Cronin states, "W aiting passively for failure is insuf ficient; but understanding these self-defeating dynamics and nudging them along through carefully targeted, synergistic counterterrorism is indispensable."[37]

This will require fortitude and patience from the people to stoically bear the vestiges of terror and its impact of life and limb of the near and dear ones. Unlike war, terror impacts the common man in the street and strikes most unexpectedly sundering normalcy peace and stability to which we are so used to. The terrorist thrives in anarchy and instability, the State must not allow such conditions to be created in its midst by exercising full legal and constitutional powers that it has including that of policing and counter rebellions. Where the state has seceded such authority over an area it has to be re-established as soon as possible. Finally given the proclivity of states to employ terror as a strategy against adversaries, cooperative mechanisms bilateral, regional and multilateral should be evolved to meet this challenge collectively, for howsoever a state may feel benefited from employing this tool as a strategy, recent history denotes that ultimately it may itself fall prey to those groups which it has fostered. With this as the backdrop we will now see the seminal event of the end of Osama Bin Laden and its impact in the succeeding chapter.

---

[37] Audrey Kurth Cronin, *How Terrorism Ends: Understanding the Decl ine and Demise of Terrorist Campaigns* . Princeton, NJ: Princeton Univ . Press, 2009. P 114 .

Chapter 3

Operation Neptune Spear

This Chapter covers Operation Neptune Spear in all its dimensions, intelligence acquisition, planning and preparations, launch as well as the aftermath including why Pakistan was not taken on board. The Conclusion suggests salient questions that the operation has raised including possibility of replication by countries other than the United States and overall influence of the death of Osama on the al Qaeda and global terrorism.

"Today, at my direction, the United S tates launched a tar geted operation against that compound, inAbbottabad, Pakistan. A small team ofAmericans carried out the operation with extraordinary courage and capability. No Americans were harmed. They took care to avoid civilian casualties. After a firefight, they killed Osama bin Laden and took custody of his body."

President Barack Obama, May 2, 2011

"This mission goes to the heart of what the CIAs all about: protectingAmerica and building a better world for our children. It demonstrates the perseverance, skill, and sheer courage of the men and women who stand watch for our nation, day in and day out.And it is a model of seamless collaboration, both within the Intelligence Community and with the US military. The material found in the compound only further confirms how important it was to go after Bin Laden. Since 9/11, this is what the American people have expected of us. In this critical operation, we delivered

Leon E. Panetta, Director of the Central Intelligence Agency.[1]

---

[1] Background Briefing with Senior Intelligence Official at the Pentagon on Intelligence Aspects of the U.S. Operation Involving Osama Bin Laden. U.S. Department of Defense Office of the Assistant Secretary of Defense (Public Affairs).

Introduction

Bin Laden the World's most wanted terrorist leader seemed to be living a charmed life till he was killed byAmerican Special Forces on 2 May 2011. In 2001, Americans launched Operation Enduring Freedom in the wake of 9/11. Rapid advance was made with a light footprint on the ground by Special Forces supported by combat aircraft and localAfghans mainly belonging to the NorthernAlliance a non Pashtun conglomerate of assorted fighters. Bin Laden escaped the noose even though the Northern Alliance was bent on retribution for targeting their hero, the Lion of PanjsherAhmad Shah Masood.

Then a few days later in Kabuls WeirAkbar Khan area on 8 November 2001, Bin Laden and the entire Al Qaeda leadership would have fallen to US air strikes. A female spy in a Burqa was bout reporting his presence to the CIA but was apprehended. Though she succeeded in sending across a message to her handlers on a satellite phone and the air strikes quickly followed, theAl Qaeda leaders had been fore warned and moved out of the location.[2]

Bin Laden and his entourage escaped into Tora Bora a labyrinth of caves on the Afghanistan Pakistan border . US Special Forces could not pursue the, "target," for a variety of operational reasons and the al Qaeda escaped by a whisker into the Kurram tribal area of Pakistan. Bin Laden however is said to have gone in a different direction to Paktia in Eastern Afghanistan and later to North Waziristan in Pakistan.

In April 2003 Bin Laden surfaced inAfghanistan after the US invasion of Iraq in the PechValley of Kunar and unfolded plans to resist theAmericans in Iraq after US Operation Iraqi Freedom had succeeded in securing Baghdad. Once again US forces were too light on the ground to have possibly discovered his move in an area which continues to be one of the favourite sanctuaries of the Taliban. In 2011 as US forces pulled out from the Pech Valley, reports indicate that there has been an influx of Al Qaeda fighters

---

[2] Osama, B efore And After , http://timesofindia.indiatimes.com/home/opinion/edit-page/Osama-Before-And-After/articleshow/8153926.cms.

there. It is possible that Bin Laden remained inAfghanistan thereafter as in 2004, he was cornered by the British in Helmand but again escaped. This was the last sign of Bin Laden's overt presence in any active area with ongoing fighting.

Given induction of NATO forces in Afghanistan starting 2006, it can be surmised that he moved out of the country and as we now know to the compound in Abbottabad in Pakistan. From this safe sanctuary he commanded his networked terrorist force through a chain of couriers who carried his directions on ten score or so pen drives.[3] Bin Laden sensed that he was safe being out of communication with the world for all practical purposes as he could not be traced electronically or physicallyThus perhaps the urge of the Thanatos let him to continue to stay in the same location for a long time allowing the United States intelligence to track him.

Bin Laden always wanted to die a martyr. The overall philosophy of the al Qaeda and Bin Laden's personal psychological proclivities indicated that he was loathe to be apprehended alive. Pakistani journalist Hamid Mir recounts Osama's repeated assertions to him in various interviews from March 1997 to November 2001. "It does not matter if I die... my death and the death of others like me will one day awaken millions of Muslims from their apathy," bin Laden told Mir in March 1997, in a cave in eastern Afghanistan's Tora Bora Mountains. In May 1998 in a hideout near Kandahar airport, he again mentioned his possible death, saying, "They cannot arrest me alive." The third time on November 8 he again said, "My martyrdom will create more Osama bin Ladens," relates Mir who was the only journalist to have interviewed Osama Bin Laden after 9/11.[4]

Bin Laden ultimately met his fate in an operation launched to track and kill him. The official code name of the mission was *Operation Neptune Spear* due to the trident spear of Neptune on the US Navy SpecialWarfare insignia. Bin Laden had the nickname *Jackpot.* The better known code

---

[3] Osama, Before And After, http://timesofindia.indiatimes.com/home/opinion/edit-page/Osama-Before-And-After/articleshow/8153926.cms

[4] Osama, Before And After, http://timesofindia.indiatimes.com/home/opinion/edit-page/Osama-Before-And-After/articleshow/8153926.cms

name *Geronimo* was for Bin Laden' s capture or death. [5] All these were symbolic codes for *Geronimo* was the famous Native American leader of the Chiricahua Apache who had defied the American government for a long time escaping the noose for a number of timesAmerican Indians were not happy with the analogy for their former hero with Bin Laden. This then was the backdrop against which *Operation Neptune Spear* to target Bin Laden was launched but it had many phases from collection of information, preparations, launching operations and the aftermath as covered in succeeding paragraphs.

Collecting Information and Intelligence

The CIA's hunt for Bin Laden commenced in 2002 and included a series of interrogations of Al Qaeda foot soldiers and later couriers on whom he relied.[6] The intelligence operation to collect information was presumably a vast enterprise given the global span of Al Qaeda. As a senior intelligence official during the back ground briefing culminating in the death of Osama Bin Laden stated, "The operation on Sunday (Monday inAbbottabad where he was killed) that resulted in the death of al Qaeda leader Osama bin Laden was a culmination of years of intelligence collection and analysis focused on disrupting, dismantling, and defeating al Qaeda". [7] The interrogation path included CIA detainees in secret prisons in Eastern Europe, eavesdropping on telephone calls and e-mails, satellite images of the compound in Abbottabad. [8]

It was a multi agency intelligence campaign to include, National Security Agency, the National Geospatial-IntelligenceAgency (NGA), ODNI [Office of the Director of National Intelligence] and the Defense Department. A

---

[5] "For God and Country Geronimo, Geronimo, Geromimo". CBN News (Christian Broadcasting Network). May 3, 2011. Retrieved May 4, 2011. Accessed through Wikipedia.

[6] Behind the hunt. http://www.indianexpress.com/news/behind-the-hunt/785395/0

[7] Background Briefing with Senior Intelligence Official at the Pentagon on Intelligence Aspects of the U.S. Operation Involving Osama Bin Laden. U.S. Department of Defense Office of the Assistant Secretary of Defense (Public Affairs)

[8] Behind the hunt. http://www.indianexpress.com/news/behind-the-hunt/785395/0

Washington post report indicated that the CIA had to go to Congress for additional funds in December 2010, "The [intelligence-gathering] effort was so extensive and costly that the CIA went to Congress in December [2010] to secure authority to reallocate tens of millions of dollars within assorted agency budgets to fund it, U.S. officials said." [9] Managing such a multi agency intelligence operation with dozens of ground agents and inputs from large number of sources globally remains a challenge for any intelligence agency including the United States. The funding for such projects will also be huge. It is unlikely that any other country apart from the United States will be able to launch such a campaign at the scale and the budget that is required.

A deductive analysis on which much intelligence relied on revealed that given the legacy and information from the ground he would be in Pakistan. This was evident from the large number of al-Qaida leaders held in Pakistan includingAbu Zubaydah, Ramzi binAl Shibh and Khalid Sheikh Mohammad. The arrest of Umar Patekone leader of bomb attacks on foreign tourists in Bali fromAbbottabad, Mullah Baradar one of the senior leaders ofTaliban from Karachi and information of entireTaliban brass holed up in Quetta were indicators that corroborated this inference as Pakistan came to be called as the headquarters of Jihad Inc. [10]

Reports now coming in denote that he may have had some links with at least one of the terrorist groups and its leader in the country without possibly giving away his location. Investigators in the United States interpreting data from seized phone of Bin Laden's trusted courier indicated that there were links with the group Harakat Ul Mujahideen. This Group is known to be a long term asset of the Pakistani intelligence agency the ISI raising questions of the possibility of some one in the agency knowing the

---

[9] Greg Mller (May 5, 2011). "CIA spied on bin Laden from safe house". *The Washington Post.* Retrieved May 6, 2011. Accessed through Wikipedia.

[10] Pak: Headquarters of Jihadis Inc.   http://lite.epaper.timesofindia.com/mobile.aspx?article=yes&pageid=13&edlabel=TOIM&mydateHid=03-05-2011&pubname=&edname=&articleid=Ar01303&format=&publabel=TOI

whereabouts of Bin Laden inAbbottabad. [11] "It's a serious lead," anAmerican official, was reported by the New York Times, "It's an avenue we're investigating." Though the intelligence officials seem to have indicated that while the Harakat had been in contact with Pakistani intelligence officials however there was no evidence to suggest that this involved information about Bin Laden. [12] Harakat "is one of the oldest and closest allies of Al Qaeda, and they are very, very close to the ISI," Bruce O. Riedel, a former Central Intelligence Agency officer and the author of " *Deadly Embrace: Pakistan, America, and the Futur e of the Global Jihad* ," was quoted by the New York Times.[13]

Harakat is also reported to have a strong network in the general area around Abbottabad thus possibly Bin Laden even if he was not in touch with the group was expecting support in some form at a pinch, one would never know. More over by locating himself in this maze of supporters, Osama was assured of a moral if not a physical support base.

More importantly in tracking a smart operator as Bin Laden who seemed to lead a benign life his vulnerabilities had to be identified. If he was able to contact the outsideWorld it would be via cell phone or email, thus hundreds and thousands of telephone connections were under surveillance. But then it was realised that he would have shifted to physical means and thus the CIA realised that Bin Laden' s vulnerability as his couriers and thus the strategy shifted to tracking these. The aim was to identify persons who facilitated him to communicate withAl Qaeda operational commanders.

The first indication of the identity of the courier was obtained in 2002, a man identified asAbu Ahmed al-Kuwaiti though the oficial name has not

---

[11] Carlotta Gall, Pir Zubair Shah and Eric Schmitt. Seized Phone Offers Clues to Bin Laden's Pakistani Links June 23, 2011. http://www.nytimes.com/2011/06/24/world/asia/24pakistan.html?_r=1

[12] Carlotta Gall, Pir Zubair Shah and Eric Schmitt. Seized Phone Offers Clues to Bin Laden's Pakistani Links June 23, 2011. http://www.nytimes.com/2011/06/24/world/asia/24pakistan.html?_r=1

[13] Carlotta Gall, Pir Zubair Shah and Eric Schmitt. Seized Phone Offers Clues to Bin Laden's Pakistani Links June 23, 2011. http://www.nytimes.com/2011/06/24/world/asia/24pakistan.html?_r=1

been revealed.[14] The name was confirmed in 2003 during the interrogation of, Khalid Sheikh Mohammed, alleged operational chief of al-Qaeda and also by a prisoner in 2004, named Hassan Ghul in Iraq, that al-Kuwaiti was close to bin Laden, Khalid Sheik Mohammed and Mohammeds successor Abu Faraj al-Libi. Gul was the first big lead toAbu Ahmed al-Kuwaiti.[15]

Both Khalid Mohammed and Abu Faraj al-Libi who was captured in May 2005 and transferred to Guantánamo in September 2006 tried to deflect the CIA by giving different information. Khalid claimed that the person was not active in Al Qaeda while Libi who did confirm that he got instruction from Bin Laden through a courier his name was Maulawi Abd al-Khaliq Jan. [16] Khalid and al-Libi both discounted al-Kuwaiti, but CIA operatives continued with the trail, possibly thinking that they had been deliberately led astray and as it appears rightly so. [17]

The first electronic link to Bin Ladens courier was obtained 8 months before the fateful raid that got the dreaded terrorist. In 2009, an ISI wiretap picked up a conversation in Arabic between a Sim card in Nowshera and another in SaudiArabia. Three months later, in 2010, the same Sim showed another conversation in Arabic, this time from Peshawar to Saudi Arabia. There were four other occasions that year when the same Sim was used, once from a location in Waziristan and the last one actually from the compound in Abbotabad, and all the transcripts and location details were passed on to the CIA.

Pakistan later claimed in a statement, "As far as the target compound is concerned, ISI had been sharing information with CIA and other friendly intelligence agencies since 2009. The intelligence flow indicating some foreigners in the surroundings ofAbbottabad continued till mid-April 2011."

---

[14] "Phone call by Kuwaiti courier led to bin Laden". *Associated Press*. May 3, 2011. Retrieved May 3, 2011. Accessed through Wikipedia.

[15] U.S. Rolled Dice in bin Laden Raid. By SIOBHAN GORMAN And ADAM ENTOUS

[16] Behind the hunt. http://www.indianexpress.com/news/behind-the-hunt/785395/0

[17] "Phone call by Kuwaiti courier led to bin Laden". *Associated Press*. May 3, 2011. Retrieved May 3, 2011.

"It is important to highlight that taking advantage of much superior technological assets, CIA exploited the intelligence leads given by us to identify and reach Osama bin Laden, a fact also acknowledged by the US President and Secretary of State in their statements," the Statement added[18].

CIA had also launched Operation Cannonball in 2005 inducting officers on the ground in Pakistan and Afghanistan. These obtained the family name of the courier which led to a trail of emails and other investigations to track him. In July 2010 the courier was spotted in Peshawar and trailed; he straight away drove to the compound in Abbottabad. [19] Physical surveillance of the house was launched from a safe house in Abbottabad using informants.

US intelligence operatives also used local help of the Pakistan police and the CID and the courier of bin Laden was apparently traced to a religious chanting group, in ascertaining addresses, verifying names and such details[20].

Through this maze of information analysts homed on to what they believed was bin Laden's safe house in Bilal Town, Abbottabad, Pakistan. Astonishingly Bin Laden was living one kilometer (0.6 mi) from Pakistans' premier military academy, and 100 kilometers (62 mi) from the capital, Islamabad. Pakistan Military Academy (PMA) is what West Point is to the United States and Sandhurst in Britain.

The Abbottabad compound was thus located in an upper class locality "The area is relatively affluent, with lots of retired military oficers. It's also insulated from the natural disasters and terrorist attacks that have afflicted other parts of Pakistan," the intelligence official briefing the media after the raid said. [21] It was a large plot of land very secluded but eight times larger than the homes in the area. There was a 12- to 18-foot outer wall with

---

[18] Carlotta Gall & Eric Schmitt.Pak hits back: Osama raid unauthorised and unilateral. Accessed through Wikipedia. http://www.indianexpress.com/news/pak-hits-back-osama-raid-unauthorised-and-unilateral/785452/0

[19] Behind the hunt. http://www.indianexpress.com/news/behind-the-hunt/785395/0

[20] US kept Pak out of loop but used local help too.

[21] How they got him: a tip-off 10 months ago, then the work and wait http://connect.in.com/barack-obama/article-how-they-got-him-a-tipoff-10-months-ago-then-the-work-and-wait-795-3b3955088bdc4d7520ab5ecb9899ed90fc1cb39a.html

barbed wire with an internal partition of more walls for extra privacy .[22] There were access control measures in terms of two security grates and no outsider was even allowed inside as the trash was also burnt by the inmates.[23] The three storey building had very few windows facing outside of the compound and even the terrace on the top had a seven-foot privacy wall.[24]

Ironically this high value property valued at approximately $1 million had no telephone or Internet connection and the owners did not seem to have any major source of income to provide for all these trappings. This led to the conclusion that this was indeed a high value custom built compound to hide some one as important as Osama. [25]

"Our best assessment, based on a large body of reporting from multiple sources, was that bin Laden was living there with several family members, including his youngest wife," the intelligence official said.[26] "Everything we saw — the extremely elaborate operational securitythe brothers' background and their behaviour, and the location and the design of the compound itself — was perfectly consistent with what our experts expected bin Laden' s hideout to look like. Keep in mind that two of bin Laden' s gatekeepers, Khalid Sheikh Mohammed and Abu Faraj al-Libbi, were arrested in the settled areas of Pakistan," he added. [27] Meanwhile a third family was also noticed to be staying in the compound and the members seemed identical to

---

[22] How they got him: a tip-off 10 months ago, then the work and wait http://connect.in.com/barack-obama/article-how-they-got-him-a-tipoff-10-months-ago-then-the-work-and-wait-795-3b3955088bdc4d7520ab5ecb9899ed90fc1cb39a.html

[23] How they got him: a tip-off 10 months ago, then the work and wait http://connect.in.com/barack-obama/article-how-they-got-him-a-tipoff-10-months-ago-then-the-work-and-wait-795-3b3955088bdc4d7520ab5ecb9899ed90fc1cb39a.html

[24] How they got him: a tip-off 10 months ago, then the work and wait http://connect.in.com/barack-obama/article-how-they-got-him-a-tipoff-10-months-ago-then-the-work-and-wait-795-3b3955088bdc4d7520ab5ecb9899ed90fc1cb39a.html

[25] How they got him: a tip-off 10 months ago, then the work and wait http://connect.in.com/barack-obama/article-how-they-got-him-a-tipoff-10-months-ago-then-the-work-and-wait-795-3b3955088bdc4d7520ab5ecb9899ed90fc1cb39a.html

[26] How they got him: a tip-off 10 months ago, then the work and wait http://connect.in.com/barack-obama/article-how-they-got-him-a-tipoff-10-months-ago-then-the-work-and-wait-795-3b3955088bdc4d7520ab5ecb9899ed90fc1cb39a.html

[27] How they got him: a tip-off 10 months ago, then the work and wait http://connect.in.com/barack-obama/article-how-they-got-him-a-tipoff-10-months-ago-then-the-work-and-wait-795-3b3955088bdc4d7520ab5ecb9899ed90fc1cb39a.html

the file on Osama's brood, which possibly clinched the issue.[28]

Security at the compound remained high as, "Despite what officials described as an extraordinarily concentrated collection effort leading up to the operation, no U.S. spy agency was ever able to capture a photograph of bin Laden at the compound before the raid or a recording of the voice of the mysterious male figure whose family occupied the structures' top two floors," indicated the intelligence official.[29] A confirmatory technique called as red teaming exercise which involved independent verification and review of all information gathered before launching the operation to ensure that it was fool proof to identify Bin Laden as no photograph of his at the compound could be found was also used.

Planning the Mission

Once the location of Osama in Abbottabad was reasonably confirmed, CIA chief Leon Panetta held a top secret meeting with President Obama, Vice President Joe Biden, Secretary of State Hillary Clinton and Defence Secretary Robert M Gates. He told the gathering that the evidence of Bin Laden's presence was some of the best that the agency had come across after Tora Bora, "best evidence since (the 2001 battle of)Tora Bora (where bin Laden was last seen), and that then makes it clear that we have an obligation to act". [30] On March 14, Panetta took the options to the White House. [31] President Obama met with his national security advisers on March 14, March 29, April 12, April 19 and April 28. Panetta gave instructions to Vice Admiral William H McRaven, commander of the Pentagon's Joint Special Operations Command (JSOC) to begin planning a military strike.[32]

---

[28] How they got him: a tip-off 10 months ago, then the work and wait http://connect.in.com/barack-obama/article-how-they-got-him-a-tipoff-10-months-ago-then-the-work-and-wait-795-3b3955088bdc4d7520ab5ecb9899ed90fc1cb39a.html

[29] Greg Miller (May 5, 2011). "CIA spied on bin Laden from saf house". The Washington Post. Retrieved May 6, 2011. Accessed through Wikipedia.

[30] Didn't tell Pak, they might have alerted targets: CIA chief http://www.expressindia.com/latest-news/Didnt-tell-Pak-they-might-have-alerted-targets-CIA-chief/785463/

[31] Behind the hunt. http://www.indianexpress.com/news/behind-the-hunt/785395/0

[32] Behind the hunt. http://www.indianexpress.com/news/behind-the-hunt/785395/0

The role of JSOC is covert operations and comprises of a number of special mission units and task forces who operate globally and are authorised by the President and report to him through the CIA Chief. Most of their missions are covert and clandestine. Many JSOC men are reported to have died in Pakistan over the past few years and have been reported as killed in Afghanistan. JSOC was thus well suited for the mission and the plan was discussed by the President on March 29 with   Vice Admiral William H. McRaven.

Three options had been discussed at the White House, a helicopter assault using American commandos, a strike with B-2 bombers that would obliterate the compound, or a joint raid with Pakistani intelligence operatives. The option to bomb was ruled out as it would require 32 bombs of 900 kg each to destroy the compound, more over confirmation of Bin Ladens'death would not be obtained. Thus gradually the Seal operation which would confirm the kill and also lead to the least amount of casualties emerged which was also facilitated by the stealth technology and particular skills that the Americans had developed. [33] The physical raid inside sovereign territory even if it is part of a coalition of sorts without informing the government is a perilous exercise. There could have been many concerns including grounding of the mission as in Iran in the 1970's. [34]

The decision was left to the President, Obama had said, "I'm not going to tell you what my decision is now — I'm going to go back and think about it some more." But he added, "I'm going to make a decision soon." "It's a go," he said finally on 29April. [35]

The instructions issued to Admiral William McRaven, head of Joint Special Forces Command by Panetta were, "to go in there (and) get bin Laden, and if bin Laden isnt there, get the hell out!"[36] Seal Team Six a part

---

[33] Behind the hunt. http://www.indianexpress.com/news/behind-the-hunt/785395/0

[34] Didn't tell Pak, they might have alerted targets: CIA chief http://www.expressindia.com/latest-news/Didnt-tell-Pak-they-might-have-alerted-targets-CIA-chief/785463/

[35] Behind the hunt. http://www.indianexpress.com/news/behind-the-hunt/785395/0

[36] Didn't tell Pak, they might have alerted targets: CIA chief http://www.expressindia.com/latest-news/Didnt-tell-Pak-they-might-have-alerted-targets-CIA-chief/785463/

of JSOC was identified to perform the task. [37] Seal Team Six is officially known as Naval SpecialWarfare Development Group.[38] Collaboration from a number of agencies was involved in planning the mission including the Technical Application Programs Of fice and the Aviation Technology Evaluation Group.[39] National SecurityAgency and the National Geospatial-Intelligence Agency also provided intimate support. [40] The Seals were provided mission simulators for the pilots by National Geospatial-Intelligence Agency and data from an RQ-170 drone.

No efforts were spared in planning and rehearsing this missionA model of the compound was reportedly created at Bagram air base and the Seals carried out extensive rehearsals on the live model. Obama' s Assistant on counterterrorism and homeland security John Brennan. "You can imagine that for something as important as this, and something as risky as this, every effort would be made to do practice runs, understand the complexities and the layout of the ground."[41] Thus Seal Team Six was fully prepared for the mission

The Operation

"Geronimo EKIA," came the crackle on the radio in the operations room, Enemy Killed in Action. President spoke up. "We got him." [42] While there was a sigh of relief for a smooth ending, the operation itself was more than

[37] Osama bin Laden dead: 40 navy commandos were training for a month http:// articles.economictimes.indiatimes.com/2011-05-03/news/29499523_1_covert-operations-seal-team-six-osama-bin

[38] Osama bin Laden dead: 40 navy commandos were training for a month http:// articles.economictimes.indiatimes.com/2011-05-03/news/29499523_1_covert-operations-seal-team-six-osama-bin

[39] Osama bin Laden dead: 40 navy commandos were training for a month http:// articles.economictimes.indiatimes.com/2011-05-03/news/29499523_1_covert-operations-seal-team-six-osama-bin

[40] Osama bin Laden dead: 40 navy commandos were training for a month http:// articles.economictimes.indiatimes.com/2011-05-03/news/29499523_1_covert-operations-seal-team-six-osama-bin

[41] US kept Pak out of loop but used local help too http://www.indianexpress.com/news/us-kept-pak-out-of-loop-but-used-local-help-too/785402/0

[42] Behind the hunt. http://www.indianexpress.com/news/behind-the-hunt/785395/0

eventful.

The aim of the operation was essentially to kill or capture Bin Laden. Senior officials however indicate that he could also have been taken alive. White House counterterrorism advisor John O. Brennan claimed that "If we had the opportunity to take bin Laden alive, if he didn't present any threat, the individuals involved were able and prepared to do that."[43] CIA Director Leon Panetta however stated on *PBS News Hour*: "The authority here was to kill bin Laden...Obviously under the rules of engagement, if he in fact had thrown up his hands, surrendered and didn't appear to be representing any kind of threat, then they were to capture him. But, they had full authority to kill him." The killing was justified as it was reported that "his wife rushed a Navy SEAL, and there was no way the SEALs could have known in that split second whether bin Laden or the room was booby-trapped in any way". [44]

79 commandos and one dog were involved in the raid. [45] The final operations were carried out by 24 [46] SEALs in two teams of 12 each. [47] SEALs were essentially equipped with M4 assault rifles, night-vision goggles and handguns. [48] The dog was a Belgian Malinois which was trained in bomb detection and named Cairo. [49] Helicopter pilots, "tactical signals, intelligence collectors, and navigators using highly classified hyper spectral

---

[43] Lynn Sweet (May 2, 2011). "Bin Laden raid: U.S. had plan to take him alive. Hiding in plan sight?". Chicago Sun-Times. Accessed through Wikipedia.

[44] Jake Tapper (May 4, 2011). "US Official: "This Was a Kill Mission"". ABC News. Accessed through Wikipedia.

[45] Myers, Steven Lee; Bumiller, Elisabeth (May 2, 2011). "Obama Calls World 'Safer' After Pakistan Raid". The New York Times. Retrieved May 3, 2011. Accessed through Wikipedia. Accessed through Wikipedia.

[46] Pierre Thomas; Martha Raddatz, Jake Tapper and Jessica Hopper (May 4, 2011). "Navy SEALs Who Captured, Killed Osama Bin Laden Return to United States". Retrieved May 4, 2011. Accessed through Wikipedia.

[47] Jim Miklaszewski (May 5, 2011). "Bn Laden 'firefight': Only one man was armed."msnbc.com. Accessed through Wikipedia.

[48] "ABC News' Kill Shot: The Story Behind bin Laden's Death". Accessed through Wikipedia.

[49] "GlobalSecurity.org: Operation Neptune Spear " Accessed through Wikipedia.

imagers" were also involved in the mission.[50] The raid had to be postponed by a day due to cloudy weather and CIA Director Leon Panetta gave the go-ahead at midday on May 1.[51]

The mission originated in Bagram with a staging forward base for the Black Hawk helicopters[52] in Jalalabad, EasternAfghanistan. The Helicopter belonged to the 160th Special Operations Aviation Regiment (SOAR), an airborne unit of the JSOC known as the Night S   talkers. Two Chinooks were also provided as a back up. Another back up force was also ready in case of a mishap.

Very low ambient light was used and helicopters used hilly terrain and nap-of-the-earth techniques to reach the compound without appearing on radar and alerting the Pakistani military. The first alarm was raised when the helicopters hovered over the compound in   Abbottabad. One of the helicopter suffered, "vortex ring state" during hovering due to the 'hot and high' environment,"[53] causing the tail to "graze one of the compound'   s walls"[54] and "breaking a rotor", but that did not deter the mission.

About 1 a.m. local time explosives were used to breach the compound walls.[55] The entry to the house was made from two directions. A top entry was made by slithering down a helicopter while ground entry was made from the ground floor The Seals team stormed the compound and a firefight broke out. Al-Kuwaiti reportedly opened fire on the first team of SEALs with an AK-47 and was killed along with his wife in the ensuing encounter . Similarly the courier's relative was shot dead before he could reach a weapon

[50] "The secret team that killed bin Laden". National Journal. May 2, 2011. Accessed through Wikipedia.

[51] Dilanian, Ken (May 2, 2011). "CIA led U.S. special forces mission against Osama bin Laden" Los Angeles Times. Accessed through Wikipedia.

[52] Max Behrman (May 2, 2011). "The Berzerker Black Hawk Helicopter That Helped Kill Osama bin Laden". Gizmodo.com. Retrieved May 12, 2011. Accessed through Wikipedia.

[53] "GlobalSecurity.org: Operation Neptune Spear" Accessed through Wikipedia.

[54] Jim Miklaszewski (May 5, 2011). "Bin Laden 'firefight': Only one man was armed"msnbc.com. Accessed through Wikipedia.

[55] Martin, David, CBS Evening News, May 3, 2011. Accessed through Wikipedia.

while Bin Laden's 22-year-old son Hamza was shot by the second team. [56/57]

Planned for 30 minutes, the raid took 38 minutes. The operation involved clearing the house from room to room securing women and children, recovering weapons and searching the compound for information. The commandos found bin Laden on the third floor and officials said he resisted before he was killed by a shot to his chest followed by one above his left eye in the "double tap," technique. [58] He had an AK-47 assault rifle and a Russian-made 9 millimeter semi-automatic Makarov pistol •500 (worth $670) and two phone numbers were discovered stitched into his clothes. [59] There are some other versions which state that bin Laden' s wife attempted to shield him and was also shot.

The Americans shot off the helicopter that had stalled and before the Pakistani forces could muster, the helicopter had left at 1.10AM local time with documents and computer hard drives leaving behind women and children. "They had no idea about who might have been on there," Brennan said. "Thankfully, there was no engagement with Pakistani forces."[60]

While bin Laden's body was taken by U.S. forces to the *Carl Vinson* in V-22 Osprey escorted by two US Navy F/A-18s.The body was measured using measurement of length of the body and Bin Laden at 6 ft 4 in (193 cm). Other bodies were left behind at the compound and later taken into Pakistani custody[61]. Finally Osama bin Laden along with his adult son (either Hamza or Khalid), Abu Ahmed al-Kuwaiti, the courier and his male relative

---

[56] Mark Landler; Mark Mazzetti (May 5, 2011). "Account Tells of One-Sided Battle in Bin Laden Raid". The New York Times. Accessed through Wikipedia.

[57] Behind the hunt. http://www.indianexpress.com/news/behind-the-hunt/785395/0

[58] Philip Sherwell (May 7, 2011). "Osama bin Laden killed: Behind the scenes of the deadly raid". The Daily Telegraph. Retrieved May 9, 2011. Accessed through Wikipedia.

[59] Christina Lamb and Nicola Smith. "Geronimo! EKIA 38 minutes to mission suc cess". The Australian. Retrieved May 12, 2011. Accessed through Wikipedia.

[60] Behind the hunt. http://www.indianexpress.com/news/behind-the-hunt/785395/0

[61] Gall, Carlotta (May 4, 2011). "Pakistani Military Investigates How Bin Laden Was Able to Hide in Plain View" . The New Y ork Times. R etrieved Ma y 4, 2011. Accessed thr ough Wikipedia.

and wife were killed in the raid.[62] A large number of computer hard drives, documents, DVDs, thumb drives, and "electronic equipment" was recovered from the site. This included 10 cell phones, five to 10 computers, 12 hard drives, at least 100 computer disks (including thumb drives and DVDs), handwritten notes, documents, weapons and "an assortment of personal items."[63] This material is stored at the FBI Laboratory in Quantico Virginia.

Osama's identity was confirmed at the compound by one of the women. Facial recognition methods were also used by CIA specialists who compared the photos of the body to known photos of Bin Laden to determine with 90 percent certainty that the body was his relying on similarity of unique features of the face such as shape and size of eyes, ears and nose. Finally separate DNA [deoxyribonucleic acid] analysis were conducted by Department of Defense and CIA labs comparing DNA profile derived from bin Laden's large extended family. "The possibility of a mistaken identity on the basis of this analysis is approximately one in 11.8 quadrillion," said the official. [64] More over the material recovered could have only been from a hide out where he was located, though the final confirmation came when the Al Qaeda acknowledged that indeed the Sheikh was dead and also that he was killed in Pakistan.[65]

Post Operation Activity

A huge cache of terrorist material, the single largest from a senior terrorist hide out was recovered in the raid. A multiagency task force to include the

---

[62] "Osama bin Laden dead: son and presumed heir also killed in aid". Daily Telegraph. May 2, 2011. Accessed through Wikipedia. & ""Osama bin Laden son disappeared during compound raid"". Telegraph.co.uk. Retrieved May 12, 2011. 7 Mark Landler; Mark Mazz etti (May 5, 2011). "Account Tells of One-Sided Battle in Bin Laden Raid"The New York Times. Accessed through Wikipedia.

[63] Bob Orr (Ma y 4, 2011). "B in Laden phone numbers help spin intel web" . CBS News. Accessed through Wikipedia.

[64] Background Briefing with Senior Intelligence Official at the Pentagon on Intelligence Aspects of the U.S. Operation Involving Osama Bin Laden. U.S. Department of Defense Office of the Assistant Secretary of Defense (Public Affairs)

[65] Background Briefing with Senior Intelligence Official at the Pentagon on Intelligence Aspects of the U.S. Operation Involving Osama Bin Laden. U.S. Department of Defense Office of the Assistant Secretary of Defense (Public Affairs)

CIA, DHS [Department of Homeland Security], DIA [Defense Intelligence Agency], the Office of the Director of National Intelligence, FBI [Federal Bureau of Investigation], the National Media Exploitation Center, NCTC [National Counterterrorism Center], NGA [National Geospatial-Intelligence Agency], NSA [National Security Agency], and Treasury was organized to decipher the material. This was in digital, audio and video files of varying sizes, printed materials, computer equipment, recording devices and handwritten documents. [66]

The initial review of the material indicated that Bin Laden had been an active leader of the Al Qaeda and had provided strategic, operational and tactical instructions to the group even though he was separated from the others. He continued to encourage plotting, inspiring and engineering acts of international terror with the USA remaining the main focus. As the intelligence official indicated, " The war against al Qaeda and its affiliates continues". [67]

There were a number of videos recovered from the compound which were released to the media.The first video was, "AMessage to theAmerican People" possibly produced sometime between October 9th and November 5th, 2010 as per the intelligence briefing. This video has not appeared so far and condemns US policy . [68] In the message to the people in the United States he is supposed to have used the favourite themes criticizing the US and capitalism. [69] In another video where Bin Laden is shown watching various video channels he has not dyed his beard indicating that he only did

---

[66] Background Briefing with Senior Intelligence Official at the Pentagon on Intelligence Aspects of the U.S. Operation Involving Osama Bin Laden. U.S. Department of Defense Office of the Assistant Secretary of Defense (Public Affairs)

[67] Background Briefing with Senior Intelligence Official at the Pentagon on Intelligence Aspects of the U.S. Operation Involving Osama Bin Laden. U.S. Department of Defense Office of the Assistant Secretary of Defense (Public Affairs)

[68] Background Briefing with Senior Intelligence Official at the Pentagon on Intelligence Aspects of the U.S. Operation Involving Osama Bin Laden. U.S. Department of Defense Office of the Assistant Secretary of Defense (Public Affairs)

[69] Background Briefing with Senior Intelligence Official at the Pentagon on Intelligence Aspects of the U.S. Operation Involving Osama Bin Laden. U.S. Department of Defense Office of the Assistant Secretary of Defense (Public Affairs)

so when he had to appear for giving various messages. [70] The intelligence officer who briefed the media thus believed that the compound inAbbottabad was an active command-and-control center for al Qaeda's top leader. [71]

The video clips seemed to determine that Osama had been obsessed with mass casualty attacks on transportation and infrastructure. There were some possible indications that he had started to recruit Americans though the intelligence officer did not confirm the same. [72]

Why Pakistan was not taken on Board?

A Question that has been debated was, why Pakistan was not on board and why was its sovereignty violated. This proved to be a controversial decision creating undercurrents of revulsion in that country particularly in theArmy. Pakistanis saw this as a clear violation of their sovereignty thereby the anti American sentiment which is generally strong in the country saw a rise.

Noted columnist of FridayTimes, Najam Sethi reports that around 1.20 am, in Rawalpindi, the DG-ISI, Lt Gen Shuja Pasha was woken up by a phone call about a crashed helicopter who in turn called up the DGMO and the COAS General Kayani to brief him who in turn called the P AF Air Chief who ordered two F-16s to scramble. CIA chief, Leon Panetta, called DG-ISI, General Pasha at 3 AM. Chairman of the Joint Chiefs of S taff Michael Mullen called Pakistan's army chiefAshfaq Parvez Kayani at about the same time to inform him of the Abbottabad Operation while President Obama called President Zardari at 7 am. Pakistani fighter jets had been scrambled when the news about a crashed helicopter was first reported.

The Americans had obviously decided not to take Pakistan on board

---

[70] Background Briefing with Senior Intelligence Official at the Pentagon on Intelligence Aspects of the U.S. Operation Involving Osama Bin Laden. U.S. Department of Defense Office of the Assistant Secretary of Defense (Public Affairs)

[71] Background Briefing with Senior Intelligence Official at the Pentagon on Intelligence Aspects of the U.S. Operation Involving Osama Bin Laden. U.S. Department of Defense Office of the Assistant Secretary of Defense (Public Affairs)

[72] Background Briefing with Senior Intelligence Official at the Pentagon on Intelligence Aspects of the U.S. Operation Involving Osama Bin Laden. U.S. Department of Defense Office of the Assistant Secretary of Defense (Public Affairs)

for the operation. CIA Director Leon Panetta told Time magazine that, "It was decided (during the planning) that any effort to work with the Pakistanis could jeopardise the mission. They might alert the targets."[73] Many raised a finger at Pakistan including US senators, counter terrorism and intelligence specialists and those from thee affected states as the India Home Minister. U.S. Senator Joe Lieberman, chairman of the Senate Homeland Security Committee, said: "This is going to be a time of real pressure on Pakistan to basically prove to us that they didn't know that bin Laden was there". [74] Senator Dianne Feinstein said that "it's hard for me to understand how the Pakistanis ... would not know what was going on inside the compound", and that top Pakistan officials may be "walking both sides of the street". Senator Lindsey Graham questioned, "How could [bin Laden] be in such a compound without being noticed?"

United States intelligence managers gave many reasons to keep Pakistan out of the loop. Pakistan's negative role in tracking down Osama previously was most prominently flagged in a Wiki leaks Cable. The missive claimed that Pakistan's security forces invariably happened to tip off the Al Qaeda chief on previous instances. Pakistan's intelligence agency is also alleged to have smuggled some of the fighters through airport security to help them escape. Even Tajikistan counter terrorism officials had indicated to the US the likely location of Osama in the past. General   Abdullo Sadulloevich Nazarov, a senior Tajik counter-terrorism official, reportedly told Americans that insiders in Pakistan knew the whereabouts of Osama Bin Laden.   [75] The Wiki Leaks cable had brought out General Nazarov's account thus, "In Pakistan, Osama bin Laden wasn't an invisible man, and many knew his whereabouts in North Waziristan, but whenever security forces attempted a raid on his hideouts, the enemy received warning of their approach from

---

[73] Didn't tell Pak, they might have alerted targets: CIA chief http://www.expressindia.com/latest-news/Didnt-tell-Pak-they-might-have-alerted-targets-CIA-chief/785463/

[74] "Pressure on P akistan after bin Laden death-lawmak er". Dawn. May 2, 2011. R etrieved May 2, 2011.

[75] Pakistan tipped Osama when US troops were near: WikiLeaks. Accessed through Wikipedia. http://www.indianexpress.com/news/pakistan-tipped-osama-when-us-troops-were-near-wikileaks/785463/

sources in the security forces." [76]

Former US national security advisor Gen James Jones even claimed that the Pakistani military knew where Osama was hiding. "My personal view is that they certainly were aware of it. For whatever reasons, they chose not to disclose it until perhaps recently. I don't know because I left the White House about six months ago. But it does raise a lot of questions, no doubt about that," Jones told the MSNBC. [77]

Pakistan has also been accused in the past of looking both ways in fighting terror most significantly by the British Prime Minister David Cameroon when he visited New Delhi in 2010. Cameroon faced a strong rebuttal from Islamabad and was virtually ostracised till he managed to assuage sentiments there and could finally visit the country in early 2011. [78]

These were possibly some of the reasons that US did not inform the Pakistani leadership in advance as the Seals descended on Abbottabad, 120 km from Islamabad. [79] Nevertheless there were other options which could have been explored such as pre-warning the highest political and military hierarchy that an operation was in the offing without actually revealing the location or the time of the same. This option was possibly ruled out due to fears that somebody in the Establishment would be in the know of Bin Laden's hiding place; therefore even a hint would give away the plot. "It's inconceivable that bin Laden did not have a support system in the country that allowed him to remain there for an extended period of time," John O Brennan, the President's top counterterrorism official, said at a White House

---

[76] Pakistan tipped Osama when US troops were near: WikiLeaks http://www.indianexpress.com/news/pakistan-tipped-osama-when-us-troops-were-near-wikileaks/785463/

[77] Pak military was aware about Osama's hiding place' http://www.indianexpress.com/news/pak-military-was-aware-about-osamas-hiding-place/785098/

[78] Pakistan tipped Osama when US troops were near: WikiLeaks http://www.indianexpress.com/news/pakistan-tipped-osama-when-us-troops-were-near-wikileaks/785463/

[79] Pakistan tipped Osama when US troops were near: WikiLeaks http://www.indianexpress.com/news/pakistan-tipped-osama-when-us-troops-were-near-wikileaks/785463/

briefing immediately following the raid.[80]"I am not going to speculate about what type of support he might have had on an official basis inside of Pakistan," he said. "We are closely talking to the Pakistanis right now, and again, we are leaving open opportunities to continue to pursue whatever leads might be out there." [81]

As also given the state of relations following the arrest and subsequent release of Mr Raymond Davis an American CIA operative in Pakistan for killing two Pakistani citizens, theAmericans possibly thought that this was not a practicable option.

What ever be the reason the outcome of the decision for not taking Pakistan on board has been disastrous for US Pakistan relations. Indian agencies are reported to have assessed that 75 percent of the Pakistani military brass are seriously concerned about the manner in which the raid was carried out by the United Sates violating sovereignty. "Only a minority (in the Pakistani military leadership) believes what the   Americans have accomplished is admirable," a source told the Indian media. "We know of such opinions, but over the coming days, this view could get further marginalized," the source said.[82] The United States hoped that with days to come this revulsion will wear of. The political impact of Osama's killing in Pakistan in the regional and internal context is being covered in detail in succeeding paragraphs.

The Reactions

The reactions to the killing of Osama were apparently mixed. First was the legality of the killing. US laws permit theAuthorization for Use of Military Force against Terrorists under the Act after September 1 1, 2001 attacks. Thus the President can use "necessary and appropriate force against those

---

[80] Didn't tell Pak, they might have alerted targets: CIA chief http://www.expressindia.com/ latest-news/Didnt-tell-Pak-they-might-have-alerted-targets-CIA-chief/785463/

[81] Didn't tell Pak, they might have alerted targets: CIA chief http://www.expressindia.com/ latest-news/Didnt-tell-Pak-they-might-have-alerted-targets-CIA-chief/785463/

[82] Pak Generals afraid US may now raid nukes http://timesofindia.indiatimes.com/india/Pak-Gens-afraid-US-may-now-raid-nukes/articleshow/8156326.cms

nations, organizations, or persons" that perpetrated 9/11 or were likely to threaten the United States. His Holiness the 14th Dalai Lama said, "Forgiveness doesn't mean forget what happened. ... If something is serious and it is necessary to take counter-measures, you have to take counter-measures."[83]

The other issue was of burial at sea. Muslim tradition requires burial within 24 hours, but by doing it at sea, American authorities presumably were trying to avoid creating a shrine for his followers. However some claim that Islamic tradition does not consider burial at sea appropriate. Mohamed Ahmed el-Tayeb, the head of Al-Azhar University, Egypt's seat of Sunni Muslim learning claimed that burial at sea was viable only when a person dies at sea. Mohammed al-Qubaisi, Dubai's grand mufti, stated: "They can say they buried him at sea, but they cannot say they did it according to Islam. If the family does not want him, it's really simple in Islam: you dig up a grave anywhere, even on a remote island, you say the prayers and that's it. Sea burials are permissible for Muslims in extraordinary circumstances. This is not one of them."Will the controversial burial at sea be used to increase antiAmerican rhetoric and propaganda by the al Qaeda in the future, it remains to be seen.

On violation of sovereignty of Pakistan again the opinions are divided. Duke University Law School Professor Scott Silliman claimed that under the international law on armed conflict and the Charter of the United Nations a foreign government can perform a military operation on a host country's soil, if the host country is not capable of and willing to deal with the problem itself.[84] Pakistan government and security agencies denied reports of providing any base to the helicopters "Reports about US helicopters taking off from Ghazi Airbase are absolutely false and incorrect. Neither any base or facility inside Pakistan was used by the US forces, nor Pakistan Army provided any operational or logistic assistance to these operations conducted

---

[83] "Dalai Lama: Speaking at USC, Dalai Lama suggests he condones Osama bin Ladenkilling". Los Angeles Times. Retrieved May 4, 2011. Accessed through Wikipedia.

[84] Searcey, Dionne (May 6, 2011). "Kiling Was Legal Under U.S. and International Law, Many Experts Say". The Wall Street Journal. Retrieved May 6, 2011. Accessed through Wikipedia.

by the US forces," had it said. [85]

A New York Times/CBS poll taken after bin Laden' s death showed that 16 percent of Americans feel safer as the result of his death while six in 10 Americans of those polled believe killing bin Laden likely would increase the threat of terrorism against the United States. Psychologists on Long Island and Oregon reported increases in people seeking treatment for anxiety and post traumatic stress syndrome. [86]

Meanwhile reactions from global leaders across the World felicitated the demise. In elaborate media briefings and speeches, the US President ensured that there was no war with Islam. "Bin Laden was not a Muslim leader; he was a mass murderer of Muslims," Obama said. "Indeed, the al-Qaeda has slaughtered scores of Muslims in many countries, including our own. So his demise should be welcomed by all who believe in peace and human dignity."[87] [88] United Nations Secretary General Ban Ki-moon called Mr. Bin Laden's death "a watershed moment in our common global fight against terrorism." Recalling being in NewYork on Sept. 11, 2001, Mr. Ban said," Personally, I am very much relieved by the news that justice has been done to such a mastermind of international terrorism." [89]

Indian Prime Minister Dr Manmohan Singh stated vide a release by his office, "I welcome it as a significant step forward and hope that it will deal a decisive blow toAl Qaeda and other terrorist groups.The international

---

[85] Carlotta Gall & Eric Schmitt.Pak hits back: Osama raid unauthorised and unilateral. http://www.indianexpress.com/news/pak-hits-back-osama-raid-unauthorised-and-unilateral/785452/0

[86] "Bin Laden death spawns new fear, dread Newsday May 8, 2011". Newsday.com. September 11, 2001. Retrieved May 11, 2011. Accessed through Wikipedia.

[87] How they got him: a tip-off 10 months ago, then the work and wait http://connect.in.com/barack-obama/article-how-they-got-him-a-tipoff-10-months-ago-then-the-work-and-wait-795-3b3955088bdc4d7520ab5ecb9899ed90fc1cb39a.html

[88] How they got him: a tip-off 10 months ago, then the work and wait http://connect.in.com/barack-obama/article-how-they-got-him-a-tipoff-10-months-ago-then-the-work-and-wait-795-3b3955088bdc4d7520ab5ecb9899ed90fc1cb39a.html

[89] World Cheers Bin Laden Killing, Prepares for Strikes http://online.wsj.com/article/SB10001424052748704569404576298362912711604.html

community and Pakistan in particular must work comprehensively to end the activities of all such groups who threaten civilized behaviour and kill innocent men, women and children." [90]

Indian Home Minister P . Chidambaram issued a statement which focused on the killing taking place deep inside Pakistan. His statement released by the Press Information Bureau read, "Earlier today the United States Government informed the Government of India that Osama Bin Laden had been killed by security forces somewhere "deep inside Pakistan.'After the September 1 1, 2001 terror attack, the US had reason to seek Osama Bin Laden and bring him and his accomplices to justice.

We take note with grave concern that part of the statement in which President Obama said that the fire fight in which Osama Bin Laden was killed took place inAbbotabad "deep inside Pakistan".This fact underlines our concern that terrorists belonging to different organisations find sanctuary in Pakistan. We believe that the perpetrators of the Mumbai terror attack, including the controllers and handlers of the terrorists who actually carried out the attack, continue to be sheltered in PakistanWe once again call upon the Government of Pakistan to arrest the persons whose names have been handed over to the Interior Minister of Pakistan as well as provide voice samples of certain persons who are suspected to be among the controllers and handlers of the terrorists." [91]

U.K. Prime Minister David Cameron, "It is a great success that he has been found and will no longer be able to pursue his campaign of global terror," Mr. Cameron said. "This is a time to remember all those murdered by Osama bin Laden, and all those who lost loved ones." [92] "His death makes the world a safer place and shows that such crimes do not remain unpunished," said European Commission President José Manuel Barroso and European Council President HermanVan Rompuy in a joint statement.

---

[90] http://pib.nic.in/newsite/erelease.aspx?relid=13656

[91] http://pib.nic.in/newsite/erelease.aspx?relid=13656

[92] World Cheers Bin Laden Killing, Prepares for Strikes http://online.wsj.com/article/SB10001424052748704569404576298362912711604.html

"This is a major achievement in our efforts to rid the world of terrorism."[93] "We can only rejoice about what happened last night," said French Finance Minister Christine Lagarde. [94]

"The state of Israel shares the joy of the   American people on this historic day of the elimination of Osama bin Laden," said a statement by Prime Minister Benjamin Netanyahu. "This is a resounding victory for justice, for freedom, and for the shared values of all democratic countries fighting shoulder to shoulder with determination against terror"[95] "Osama bin Laden was one of the most brutal terrorists in the world. He had the lives of thousands of innocent people on his conscience," German Foreign Minister Guido Westerwelle said in an emailed statement. [96] From the Philippines, "The death of Osama bin Laden should not lull us into complacency" said President Benigno Aquino III in a statement. "The world must continue to consistently and courageously raise its collective voice against religious hatred, political intolerance, and terrorism of all kinds."[97]

From the Islamic World there was not as much joy. Turkish President Abdullah Gul also hailed the news.   A Saudi official said he hoped that "elimination of al-Qaeda leader is a step towards combating terrorism, dismantling its cells, and destroying the deviant ideology and those who support it." [98] Many other   Arab governments did not publish official's statements, but officials reportedly indicated that they celebrated Mr. Bin Laden's demise. [99] In Gaza, Hamas leaders condemned the killing. "Killing

[93] World Cheers Bin Laden Killing, Prepares for Strikes http://online.wsj.com/article/SB10001424052748704569404576298362912711604.html

[94] World Cheers Bin Laden Killing, Prepares for Strikes http://online.wsj.com/article/SB10001424052748704569404576298362912711604.html

[95] World Cheers Bin Laden Killing, Prepares for Strikes http://online.wsj.com/article/SB10001424052748704569404576298362912711604.html

[96] World Cheers Bin Laden Killing, Prepares for Strikes http://online.wsj.com/article/SB10001424052748704569404576298362912711604.html

[97] World Cheers Bin Laden Killing, Prepares for Strikes http://online.wsj.com/article/SB10001424052748704569404576298362912711604.html

[98] World Cheers Bin Laden Killing, Prepares for Strikes http://online.wsj.com/article/SB10001424052748704569404576298362912711604.html

[99] World Cheers Bin Laden Killing, Prepares for Strikes http://online.wsj.com/article/SB10001424052748704569404576298362912711604.html

Osama Bin Laden is a continuation of the U.S. policy of oppression. We condemn the assassination of a Muslim mujahed," Mr . Haniyeh said. [100] The statement came even as the Hamas wants to separate itself from al Qaeda's ideology of global jihad. [101]

The Muslim Brotherhood, Egypt's most powerful Islamist political group, condemned the assassination of Mr. Bin Laden. [102] In Pakistan hundreds of activists of Jamaat-ud-Dawa (JuD), offered funeral prayers for Osama bin Laden in Karachi, calling him a "martyr of Islam". [103]

On the whole as well the death of Osama Bin Laden may be the beginning of a new phase for while the   Americans have rejoiced those outside American haven't and may seek justice in the days ahead. [104] "His martyrdom has the potential to reinvigorate al Qaeda's brand among those already radicalized to the cause," said Leah Farrall, an   Australian counterterrorism expert who has carried out a detailed study of the Al Qaeda has remarked. [105]

Al Qaeda Reacts to Bin Laden's Death

Shiraz Maher, a Senior Fellow at the International Centre for the Study of Radicalisation (ICSR) at King's College London who has been monitoring internet forums linked to the al Qaeda finds it intriguing that the group which is generally quick in announcing deaths of its leaders such as Abu Musab al-Zarqawi, the leader of al Qaeda in Iraq in 2006 or Mustafa Abu al-Yazid, al Qaeda's alleged financial chief, in a drone strike in Pakistan in 2010 did not

---

[100] World Cheers Bin Laden Killing, Prepares for Strikes http://online.wsj.com/article/ SB10001424052748704569404576298362912711604.html

[101] World Cheers Bin Laden Killing, Prepares for Strikes http://online.wsj.com/article/ SB10001424052748704569404576298362912711604.html

[102] World Cheers Bin Laden Killing, Prepares for Strikes http://online.wsj.com/article/ SB10001424052748704569404576298362912711604.html

[103] Hundreds join JuD prayers for 'martyr' Osama http://www.indianexpress.com/news/ hundreds-join-jud-prayers-for-martyr-osama/785406/0

[104] Osama, Before And After http://timesofindia.indiatimes.com/home/opinion/edit-page/ Osama-Before-And-After/articleshow/8153926.cms.

[105] U.S. to Probe Pakistan Support for bin Laden. http://online.wsj.com/article/ SB10001424052748704569404576299500647391240.html

react to Bin Laden's death for four days.[106] This possibly demonstrated the sense of shock and disbelief in the organization.

But when the flow of responses started al Qaeda's reactions to the death of the leader or Amir send a clear message of retribution. The first major Al Qaeda statement came on 6 May 2011 in a four page statement the release noted, "[Bin Laden] was killed in truth in a situation of truth." "We in al Qaeda organisation pledge to Allah the almighty and ask his help, support and steadfastness to continue on the path of jihad, the path walked upon by our leaders, and on top of them, Sheikh Osama," US Monitoring Group SITE intelligence report quoted the statement. "We also stress that the blood of the mujahid Sheikh Osama bin Laden, may Allah have mercy upon him, weighs more to us and is more precious to us and to every Muslim than to be wasted in vain," it said.[107]

Then it went on to raise a cry for revenge thus, "So if the Americans were able to kill Usama, this is not shame or stigma. But can the Americans, with their media, agents, machinery soldiers, intelligence and agencies kill that for which Sheikh Usama lived and that for which he was killed?"

Ayman al Zawahiri, possibly the man closest to Bin Laden issued a statement only after he was officially anointed the leader on 16 June 2011. In a 28-minute long video eulogy to Osama bin Laden, titled "The Noble Knight Dismounted" Zawahiri said, "The man who terrified America in his life will continue to terrify it after his death… You will continue to be troubled by his famous vow: You shall not dream of security until we enjoy it and until you depart the Muslims' lands."

The al Qaeda branches, al Qaeda in Iraq, and al Qaeda in the Islamic Maghreb issued official statements, while others such as Jemaah Islamiyah's spiritual leader, were to an extent spontaneous. Abu Bakr al Baghdad al Qurashi, the leader of al Qaeda in Iraq threatened to go on the offensive

---

[106] Shir az Maher. Islamist W eb Sites and The Future of Al Qaeda. http://www.foreignaffairs.com/articles/67841/shiraz-maher/jihadis-react-to-bin-ladens-death

[107] Al Qaeda confirms Osama bin Laden's death. Available at http://www.dawn.com/2011/05/06/al-qaeda-confirms-osama-bin-ladens-death.html

and said, his group will not "sit idly by crying like women." Adding, "So sleep soundly O Lion of Islam and Sheikh of the Mujahideen (holy warrior), for we are not of those who shed tears and sit idly by crying like women — this was not and will not be our way ," according to an English-language translation by SITE. He also promised allegiance of his group to Ayman al-Zawahiri being possibly the first to indicate the most likely successor

The Al Qaeda in the Islamic Maghreb related the death to the Arab Spring thus, "Everyone testifies ... that these events that are storming through the Arab region are only a fruit among the fruits of jihad in which the sheikh (bin Laden) had a prominent role," according to a translation by SITE Intelligence Group. Jemaah Islamiyah founder and spiritual leader Abu Bakir Bashir before going on a trial for supporting an al Qaeda cell in Aceh stated, "I don't know if it's true, but if he is dead, God willing he will go to heaven." Bashir shrewdly denied that he ahd any links with the Al Qaeda or Bin Laden. [108]

Internet forums which are the main medium to spread extremist messages were active with Bin Laden's videos, "And Incite the Believers" and replication of, "blessed Manhattan raid," or 9/1. [109] Some announcements were chilling with threats to launch attacks on the United States that "will even make the hair of babies turn grey."[110] The forums were also used by the Group to eulogize the leader and attract potential recruits particularly indicating that paradise is the path to which the slain commander has gone and that is what others should aspire for. Thus in many ways Bin Laden's death was used to expand the base of support rather than weeping or wailing over the leader. [111] This was also a psychological prop to call for retribution and boost up morale through fiery proclamations.

[108] Bill Roggio. Al Qaeda affiliates weigh in on Osama bin Laden's death. May 9, 2011. http://www.longwarjournal.org/threat-matrix/archives/2011/05/al_qaeda_affiliates_weigh_in_o.php#ixzz1MFOKFBHF

[109] Shiraz Maher. Islamist Web Sites and The Future of Al Qaeda. http:// www .foreignaffairs.com/articles/67841/shiraz-maher/jihadis-react-to-bin-ladens-death

[110] Shiraz Maher. Islamist Web Sites and The Future of Al Qaeda. http:// www .foreignaffairs.com/articles/67841/shiraz-maher/jihadis-react-to-bin-ladens-death

[111] Shiraz Maher. Islamist Web Sites and The Future of Al Qaeda. ht tp:/www.foreignaffairs.com/ articles/67841/shiraz-maher/jihadis-react-to-bin-ladens-death

Concluding Remarks –A Unique or One off Incident

Operation Neptune Spear which led to the death of Osama Bin Laden in a compound in Abbottabad, Pakistan is a unique event in the history of global counter terrorism. It has many nuances of a sustained intelligence campaign employing a variety of means, human and technical carried out with exceptional security. The operation was meticulously planned once again with the best possible technology available including stealth, helicopter and storming of a virtual citadel in the dark of the night in alien country   . It demonstrated the best human skills in all spheres. The mission was achieved with no harm coming to the crew while causing minimum collateral damage. Undoubtedly it will go down as the finest success in clandestine operations.

A question arises whether this mission can be replicated by the Americans or by any other country. The answer to the first part appears to be a possible yes while the second a definite no. The reasons for the latter being as follows:-

(a) The scale of information and intelligence that is desired for such missions is presently available only with the United States; no other country seems to be even remotely near such a possibility.

(b) The capability to launch clandestine and covert operations that rests with the USOC is also unique.

(c) More over apart from the US, violation of sovereignty of a country as large as Pakistan armed with nuclear weapons may not be seen as practicable by any other state. Even in this case the effect of this violation are yet to be fully gauged as the same may dampen the overall aim of stability in Af-Pak in the short to medium term.

There are other questions on the impact of the killing of Osama on the al Qaeda and global terrorism which will be explored in the succeeding chapters in detail to include the following:-

(a) How has the Al Qaeda being affected by the decapacitation of Bin Laden? Will an or ganisation of its spatial spread be neutralised after the death of its principal leader?

(b) What will be the trajectory of the al Qaeda and terrorism thus? Can Ayman al Zawahiri regroup and reorganise the organisation and sustain its objective?

(c) How will the branches of al Qaeda and its affiliates as the Lashkar e Taiyyaba or as Shabab be impacted?

(d) What would be the response from states that have provided sanctuaries willingly or unwillingly to terrorist groups as the al Qaeda?

(e) What would be a viable strategy (s) to meet the challenge from terrorism thus?

Chapter 4

Al Qaeda Beyond Bin Laden

This Chapter examines the impact of Bin Laden' s death on the Al Qaeda by examining the background of the myth that led to his rise in the global terrorism hierar chy, or ganisation and functioning of the gr oup, the changes that have come about in the past and how the rise ofAyman al Zawahiri is likely to impact the group. In the light of above thoughts by some prominent analysts on how the Al Qaeda's end can be brought about have been examined.

Introduction

Most counter terrorism specialists agree that the death of Bin Laden is likely to be a seminal benchmark in the history of global terrorism as well as the al Qaeda, however it is unlikely to be the end of the organization or the movement of radicalization set off by his ideology. While Bin Laden as is now revealed was providing what in military terms is called as, "directional," leadership to the organization for the past decade or so, the organization has only grown from the backwaters of Afghanistan and Pakistan to Yemen, Iraq and Algeria where three branches have flourished over the years. Its affiliates as the Lashkar e Taiyyaba have successfully carried out complex terrorist attacks as that in Mumbai on 26 November 201 1 replicating Al Qaeda's core expertise.Al Qaeda is also continuously focused on attacking the United S tates and under Bin Laden' s leadership was planning and preparing for another catastrophic 9/11 replication which fortunately never came through.

The organization has seen a some what smooth transition of leadership to the second in command, Zawahiri who is well versed with the functioning and strategies of the network and is also known to be a very dangerous foe. He has the organizational capability and strength of will to sustain the group over a period. Will Ayman Zawahiri succeed where Bin Laden failed in targeting the United States once again remains to be seen?

It can be however presumed that theAl Qaeda may continue activities in Afghanistan and Pakistan, West Asia and North Africa where it has a terror footprint, while planning for a strike in mainland USA or in Europe. In the immediate term the focus of Zawahiri will be survival. The Egyptian doctor will naturally be on the priority list of the United States and the longer the new leadership structure under him gets time to settle down the greater would be the danger . In the medium to long term however it would be necessary to adopt a holistic strategy to not just neutralize the organization but also diffuse its ideological impact across theWorld. An overview of the Bin Laden's life and influences, the al Qaeda today and likely future is provided as per succeeding paragraphs.

The Myth and Reality of Osama Bin Laden

Osama's Background: How it inspir es his ilk?

To understand the attraction of Bin Laden to a core section of the Muslim youth across the World including the United S tates and Europe there is a need to examine his background. Born with a silver spoon in a wealthy Saudi family, Osama is seen to have shed his preferential upbringing for a life in the caves of Afghanistan. This is the simplistic version which was pandered around to demonstrate his attachment and fervour to the cause. The larger perspective however demystifies the al Qaeda leader.

Osama bin Muhammad binAwad bin Laden was born in 1957, seventh son and 17th child, among 50 or more, of his fatherSteve Coll, in his book "*The Bin Ladens: An Arabian Family in the American Century,*" indicates that Bin Laden said he was born in January 1958.[1] His family belonged to

---

[1] The most wanted face of terrorism Al-Qaida leaders killed or captured since 9/11. http://

Southern Yemen and his father had moved to Jeddah to work as a porter for the Hajj pilgrims on their way to the holy city of Mecca. Laden senior went on to create the lar gest construction company in Saudi Arabia built on lucrative contracts that the Saudi government had to dEr through oil money.[2] Bin Laden's father soon became the preferred contractor for the House of Saud in the 1950s earning a fortune building palaces and renovating even the Dome of the Rock and the Al Aqsa mosque in Jerusalem. When his father died in 1967 in a plane crash, Osama meaning, "young lion," was 10 and had a privileged childhood, playing with Saudi princes.[3] His inheritance of the vast fortune of his father was to fund the al Qaeda in the future.

Osama seems to have suffered some discrimination as his mother was a Syrian and he was her only child and was possibly seen as an outsider by the larger Bin Laden family. Mary Anne Weaver writing in the New Yorker quotes a family friend to suggest that he may have been some what ostracised in his own family. "It must have been difficult for him," the family friend said. "Osama was almost a double outsiderHis paternal roots are inYemen, and within the family his mother was a double outsider as well — she was neither Saudi nor Yemeni but Syrian."[4]

He was also the only Bin Laden siblings who never travelled abroad to study. Thus while his other brothers went on to live in the UnitedtStes and took up Western vocations benefiting from the huge fortune inherited from their father Bin Laden seemed to have developed a hatred for theWest and embraced Wahhabism.

---

www.nytimes.com/2011/05/02/world/02osama-bin-laden-obituary.html?pagewanted=6&hp

[2] The most wanted face of terrorism Al-Qaida leaders killed or captured since 9/11. http://www.nytimes.com/2011/05/02/world/02osama-bin-laden-obituary.html?pagewanted=6&hp

[3] The most wanted face of terrorism Al-Qaida leaders killed or captured since 9/11. http://www.nytimes.com/2011/05/02/world/02osama-bin-laden-obituary.html?pagewanted=6&hp

[4] The most wanted face of terrorism Al-Qaida leaders killed or captured since 9/11. http://www.nytimes.com/2011/05/02/world/02osama-bin-laden-obituary.html?pagewanted=6&hp

During his period of education at the KingAbdulaziz University in Jidda he was also exposed to the Muslim Brotherhood which advocated a puritanical strain of Islam then. [5] Those who had a great influence on Bin Laden then were Islamic scholars: Muhammad Quttub andAbdullah Azzam. "Jihad and the rifle alone: no negotiations, no conferences and no dialogue," was whatAzzam taught Bin Laden and the terrorist leader seemed to follow these instructions in letter and spirit.   JordanianAbu Muhammad al-Maqdisi a Salafist cleric is another fundamentalist cleric who has immense influence on Al Qaeda ideology. [6] There is no doubt then that the upbringing of the man had very major influence on the path of terrorism in the years ahead.

The Beginnings of a GlobalTerrorist

Ironically it was the Saudi government who decided to despatch Bin Laden to Afghanistan to support the resistance movement when the Soviets entered the country in 1979.At this stage his role was that of a government emissary rather than a revolutionary. [7] Slowly and gradually he converted to a radical rebel leader setting up guest houses for fighters streaming from across the Arab world in Peshawar , Pakistan. Then the Of fice of Services was established to channelize the movement of fighters and the mujahedeen campaign against the Soviets began where Bin Laden learnt the ropes of fostering insurgency. [8] The Al Qaeda and Bin Laden unlike what is popularly believed did not play a major role in the   Afghan war. Possibly here Bin Laden recognized limitations of conducting militancy without state support and may have thus turned towards terrorism as a focal strategy for the

---

[5] The most wanted face of terrorism Al-Qaida leaders killed or captured since 9/11. http://www.nytimes.com/2011/05/02/world/02osama-bin-laden-obituary.html?pagewanted=6&hp

[6] Brynjar Lia. Al Qaeda Wi thout Bin Laden. How Terrorists Cope With their Leader's Death. http://www.foreignaffairs.com/articles/67846/brynjar-lia/al-qaeda-without-bin-laden

[7] The most wanted face of terrorism Al-Qaida leaders killed or captured since 9/11. http://www.nytimes.com/2011/05/02/world/02osama-bin-laden-obituary.html?pagewanted=6&hp

[8] The most wanted face of terrorism Al-Qaida leaders killed or captured since 9/11. http://www.nytimes.com/2011/05/02/world/02osama-bin-laden-obituary.html?pagewanted=6&hp

group, but these are surmises.

During the early years after the Soviets left, Bin Laden's group remained small and had suffered many desertions as well as deaths. By mid-1996, al Qaeda was reduced to some 30 members. Faced with virtual extinction he declared war on the United States. In 1998, bin Laden used his newly created World Islamic Front for Jihad Against Jews and Crusaders to lobby other groups to join him. [9] Bin Laden then adopted the strategy of mass impact attacks against the US to attract followers. [10] Al Qaeda also developed a common ideology or *manhaj* (program) to build lasting unity and an open front to attract new fighters. [11]

By 2001, al Qaeda included a core of just under 200 people, a 122-person martyrdom brigade, and several dozen foot soldiers recruited from the 700 or so graduates in its training camps though all this had made it the strongest of the 14 foreign militant groups operating in Afghanistan then under the Taliban. [12] The mid-2001 merger of the al Qaeda with Egyptian Islamic Jihad, led byAyman al-Zawahiri, who has now taken over al Qaeda, provided it the mass. 9/11 was its defining moment, an event designed as Bin Laden had always hoped it would to pitch fork his group on the global stage. Yet some would say it was also a personal doom for him having been hounded from one cave to another, one hide out to another.

9/11 was a seminal event and brought together a diverse group of countries across the globe to counter the threat from Al Qaeda including Saudi Arabia and Egypt who possibly envisaged a major danger from Bin Laden's proliferation but also other states as diverse as Kenya and Malaysia. Operation Enduring Freedom did not mark the end of Al Qaeda but only a

---

[9] Leah Farrall. How Al Qaeda Works? Foreign Affairs. March/April 2011. ht tp:// www.foreignaffairs.com/articles/67467/leah-farrall/how-al-qaeda-works

[10] Leah Farrall. How Al Qaeda Works? Foreign Affairs. March/April 2011. ht tp:// www.foreignaffairs.com/articles/67467/leah-farrall/how-al-qaeda-works

[11] Leah Farrall. How Al Qaeda Works? Foreign Affairs. March/April 2011. http:// www.foreignaffairs.com/articles/67467/leah-farrall/how-al-qaeda-works

[12] Leah Farrall. How Al Qaeda Works? Foreign Affairs. March/April 2011. http:// www.foreignaffairs.com/articles/67467/leah-farrall/how-al-qaeda-works http:// online.wsj.com/article/SB10001424052748704569404576299500647391240.html

transition to a different form. Thus November 2001 sawAl Qaeda morphing into smaller nodes which could to carry out strikes on their own weaved into a larger network. From a hierarchical organisation it assumed a directive one.[13]

The Al Qaeda rejuvenated itself from 2004 to 2006 but drone operations in north Waziristan have again put the oganization under pressure and there have been instances of delegation of operational responsibility toAl Qaeda in theArabian Peninsula (AQAP) andAl Qaeda in Iraq (AQI) in particular[14]

On the other hand the unprecedented threat viewed from non state actors possibly led to states cooperating across the spectrum of international politics an era which RichardA. Falkenrath feels may come to an end with the death of Bin Laden. Many mark this as diffusion of terrorism as a security threat across the globe. Revulsion of US policy of counter terrorism in countries as Pakistan is a similar challenge that will prevent taking the decapacitation of the leader to the logical conclusion of exterminating the organization as well as the base of terrorism.[15]

Why Bin LadenWas Underestimated?

Bin Laden was in many ways the most underestimated terrorist leader before 9/11. This was perhaps the main failing of the intelligence community before and even after the attack onWorld Trade Towers till he was finally tracked down and killed on 2 May 2011.

A review of his statements reflecting his ideology would indicate the deep and ingrained sense of hatred that he had against the United States and its allies. "It (America) wants to occupy our countries, steal our resources, impose agents on us to rule us and then wants us to agree to all this," Osama Bin Laden to CNN in a 1997 interview"If we refuse to do so,

---

[13] U.S. to Probe Pakistan Support for bin Laden. http://online.wsj.com/article/SB1000142 4052748704569404576299500647391240.html

[14] Leah F arrall. How Al Qaeda W orks? F oreign Af fairs. Mar ch/April 2011. ht tp:// www.foreignaffairs.com/articles/67467/leah-farrall/how-al-qaeda-works

[15] Richard A. Falkenrath. Was Bin Laden the Easy Part? http:www.foreignaffairs.com/articles/ 67831/richard-a-falkenrath/was-bin-laden-the-easy-part

it says we are terrorists. When Palestinian children throw stones against the Israeli occupation, the U.S. says they are terrorists. Whereas when Israel bombed the United Nations building in Lebanon while it was full of children and women, the U.S. stopped any plan to condemn Israel. At the same time that they condemn any Muslim who calls for his rights, they receive the top official of the Irish RepublicanArmy at the White House as a political leader . Wherever we look, we find the U.S. as the leader of terrorism and crime in the world." [16]   In February 1998, he had declared that every Muslim had a duty to "killAmericans wherever they are found."[17] "I am confident that Muslims will be able to end the legend of the so-called superpower that is America," said Osama. [18]

Then the series of attacks against US facilities across the Middle East should have indicated his focus. The first attack on World Trade Center, in 1993; bombing of the Khobar Towers in Saudi Arabia; and a foiled plot to hijack a dozen jets, crash a plane into the C.I.A. headquarters and kill then US President Bill Clinton were the main acts or attempts attributable to Osama Bin Laden before 9/11. He was also involved in bombings of two American embassies in EastAfrica in August 1998, this was when then US President Clinton declared Bin Laden "Public Enemy No. 1."

Bin Laden consistently used public speeches to issue orders for attack such as the one onWestern oil supply routes in the Gulf in 2004. In 2006 and 2008 he reportedly ordered the attack on the artist who created the caricature of Muhammad first published in Denmark's Jyllands-Posten. In 2007 and 2009, he sent the call for supporting Somalia and in January of 201 he sent an audio message for the release of French hostages by al Qaeda in the

---

[16] The most wanted face of terrorism Al-Qaida leaders killed or captured since 9/11. http://www.nytimes.com/2011/05/02/world/02osama-bin-laden-obituary.html?pagewanted=6&hp

[17] The most wanted face of terrorism Al-Qaida leaders killed or captured since 9/11. http://www.nytimes.com/2011/05/02/world/02osama-bin-laden-obituary.html?pagewanted=6&hp

[18] The most wanted face of terrorism Al-Qaida leaders killed or captured since 9/11. http://www.nytimes.com/2011/05/02/world/02osama-bin-laden-obituary.html?pagewanted=6&hp

Islamic Maghreb (AQIM).[19] Leah Farral, a former Senior Counterterrorism Intelligence Analyst with the Australian Federal Police and the author of the blog All Things Counter Terrorism feels that "Today, it has more members, greater geographic reach, and a level of ideological sophistication and influence it lacked ten years ago".[20]

Then he was not ordinary terrorist leader. Hounded by almost every intelligence agency of the West and also not provided shelter in any state at least overtly, he succeeded in remaining in touch with his organization for a decade. Bin Laden is reported to have used innovative methods to stay in touch with his organization. He would type messages on his computer,copy the file into a thumb drive and then through a courier have it transmitted through an internet café far away from his hide out. The courier would download messages from the internet on the flash drive and bring it back to Bin Laden, thereby not requiring an internet connection while still remaining in touch and guiding and organizing his Group.[21] A detailed study of these incidents would have indicated that he was a dangerous terrorist's leader whose main goal was to carry out mass suicide attacks with America as the main focus.[22]

Impact of Bin Laden's Death on Al Qaeda

The main impact of Bin Laden's death on Al Qaeda was to breach the aura of invincibility that he had build around himself.At the same time martyrdom expanded the halo, thus the long term influence may be difficult to judge at present. From the intelligence point of view information that was available

---

[19] Brynjar Lia. Al Qaeda Without Bin Laden. How Terrorists Cope With their Leader's Death. http://www.foreignaffairs.com/articles/67846/brynjar-lia/al-qaeda-without-bin-laden

[20] Leah Farrall. How Al Qaeda Works? Foreign Affairs. March/April 2011. http://www.foreignaffairs.com/articles/67467/leah-farrall/how-al-qaeda-works

[21] Thomas Joscelyn. Osama bin Laden's Internet connection. May 12, 2011. http://www.longwarjournal.org/threat-matrix/archives/2011/05/ap_how_osama_bin_laden_emailed.php#ixzz1MF0VkQbw

[22] The most wanted face of terrorism Al-Qaida leaders killed or captured since 9/11. http://www.nytimes.com/2011/05/02/world/02osama-bin-laden-obituary.html?pagewanted=6&hp

on his computers and pen drives is likely to be useful for targeting the group depending on how the American agencies make use of the same. If this does contain information of value and is correctly interpreted, then this can provide a number of leads to other leaders, provided the same is exploited very rapidly before they change their alibis, hide outs, methods of communication and operations.[23] In June 2011 this may already be too late.

Leah Farral, Australian counter terror expert on Al Qaeda states, the impact of Bin Laden or even Zawahiri's death will not be grave on the organization. "Because al Qaeda's second-tier leadership manages most of the group's interaction with its subsidiaries, the removal of either Zawahiri or bin Laden would not overly af fect the unity among the or ganization's core, branch, and franchises, nor would it impede communication among them," she states.[24] In a similar vein counter terrorism expert Bruce Hoffman argues, al Qaeda is "in the main flatter,more linear, and more organizationally networked" than it has previously been. Killing of bin Laden may as per Hoffman increase the pace of decentralization. [25]

Apart from the vast spread across South and West Asia, the al Qaeda is likely to retain support of the Pashtun networks in the tribal areas of Af Pak as these linkages go back into history for many years and are deeper than that with groups in Yemen or in Somalia. [26] The continuing global support base for the Al Qaeda with a stream of willing volunteers arriving every week indicates that there is no dearth of new recruits. "So many people arrive every month that there are problems finding places for them to stay," Rami Makanesi, a suspected al-Qaida member from Hambur g

---

[23] Brynjar Lia. Al Qaeda Without Bin Laden. How Terrorists Cope With their Leader's Death. http://www.foreignaffairs.com/articles/67846/brynjar-lia/al-qaeda-without-bin-laden

[24] Leah Farrall. How Al Qaeda W orks? Foreign Af fairs. Mar ch/April 2011. ht tp:// www.foreignaffairs.com/articles/67467/leah-farrall/how-al-qaeda-works

[25] Seth G Jones. The Al Qaeda Thr eat in Pakistan. Testimony presented bef ore the House Homeland Security Committee, Subcommittee on Counterterrorism and Intelligence on May 3, 2011. RAND Corporation. Santa Monica. 2011

[26] Seth G Jones. The Al Qaeda Thr eat in Pakistan. Testimony presented bef ore the House Homeland Security Committee, Subcommittee on Counterterrorism and Intelligence on May 3, 2011. RAND Corporation. Santa Monica. 2011

was reported by the media. [27] Some of the proliferation has seen establishment of camps and villages with the name, "GermanTaliban," and, "European Taliban," Islamic Mujahideen of Uzbekistan and its of fshoot, Islamic Jihad Union (IMU and the IJU) have large numbers of Germans and European members. IMU camps are located in Samangan, Balkh, and Sar-i-Pul provinces of Afghanistan. [28]

In one scenario theAl Qaeda could crumble as Bin Laden had become a symbol larger than the group itself, however at the other end of the spectrum the decentralization that it has achieved over a period may lead to rejuvenation thereby requiring greater focus on territorial control and counter terrorism cooperation in a number of countries, Afghanistan, Pakistan and Yemen being the priority. [29] The larger ideological movement is likely to continue as perceived grievances of against the West are not likely to go away. [30]

Al Qaeda – The Base

The Organisation

The present organization of the al Qaeda can be divided into five tiers: "central al Qaeda, affiliated groups, allied groups, allied networks, and inspired individuals". Al Qaeda Central is presently based in Af Pak tribal area but the location need not be specific to an area particularly as the command and control is diffused in several nodes across South andWest Asia. The affiliated groups are the Al Qaeda in Iraq, Al Qaeda in the Arabian Peninsula, Al Qaeda in the Islamic Maghreb, and Al Qaeda East Africa who use the

---

[27] Bill Roggio. Business is still booming at Afghan and Pakistani terror camps May 10, 2011. http://www.longwarjournal.org/threat-matrix/archives/2011/05/business_is_still_booming_at_a.php#ixzz1MFOo9mvk May 10, 2011. http://www.longwarjournal.org/threat-matrix/archives/2011/05/business_is_still_booming_at_a.php#ixzz1MFOo9mvk

[28] Ibid.

[29] Alexander Gallo and Scott Helfstein. Springtime for Jihadis. How Will Terrorism Evolve After Bin Laden? http://www.foreignaffairs.com/articles/67839/alexander-gallo-and-scott-helfstein/springtime-for-jihadis

[30] Brynjar Lia. Al Qaeda Without Bin Laden. How Terrorists Cope With their Leader's Death. http://www.foreignaffairs.com/articles/67846/brynjar-lia/al-qaeda-without-bin-laden

prefix to their name.[31] They differ from the allied groups in that their overall direction rests with the al Qaeda central leadership particularly in terms of nomination of commanders, engaging varied types of targets and conduct of attacks outside their normal area of influence. The allied groups are not required to take any direction from Al Qaeda central and carry out activities restricted to local goals and objectives in areas of influence Tehrik-e-Taliban Pakistan and Lashkar-e-Tayyiba are two examples along with as Shabaab in Somalia. In the fourth tier are smaller groups and individuals directly connected to the Al Qaeda with terrorism experience or even those who have partaken training in the camps in Af Pak. [32]

Professor Rohan Gunaratna well known counter terrorism commentator in a RSIS Commentary on May 3 indicates the importance of Bin Laden as the one who could bring together a number of like minded leaders and groups in a conflict to form an alliance[33] It is not important for these groups to formally be part of the al Qaeda network, they have to only have filial loyalty and cooperate to achieve the common goal. In that sense the al Qaeda was truly, "The Base". Some of the groups associated to the al Qaeda though not necessarily forming a part of its formal network over the years are as follows[34]:-

---

[31] Seth G Jones. The Al Qaeda Thr eat in Pakistan. Testimony presented before the House Homeland Security Committee, Subcommittee on Counterterrorism and Intelligence on May 3, 2011. RAND Corporation. Santa Monica. 2011

[32] Seth G Jones. The Al Qaeda Thr eat in Pakistan. Testimony presented before the House Homeland Security Committee, Subcommittee on Counterterrorism and Intelligence on May 3, 2011. RAND Corporation. Santa Monica. 2011

[33] James Veitch and John Martin. The Death of Osama Bin Laden and the Future of Al Qaeda. Bangladesh Institute of Peace and Security Studies. Dhaka 2011.

[34] James Veitch and John Martin. The Death of Osama Bin Laden and the Future of Al Qaeda. Bangladesh Institute of Peace and Security Studies. Dhaka 2011.

•	Armed Islamic Group (Algeria)	•	Harakat ul Ansar/Mujahadeen (Pakistan)
•	Salafist Group for Call and Combat and the Armed Islamic Group- (GSPC) (Algeria) – Morphed into Al Qaeda of the Islamic Maghreb	•	Harakat ul Jihad (Kashmir/India/Pakistan)
•	Egyptian Islamic Jihad (Egypt)	•	Jamiat Ulema-e-Islam (Pakistan)
•	Al-Gama'a al-Islamiyya (Egypt)	•	Jamiat-ul-Ulema-e-Pakistan
•	Jamaat Islamiyya (Indonesia)	•	Moro Islamic Liberation Front (Philippines)
•	The Libyan Islamic Fighting Group	•	Abu Sayyaf Group (Malaysia, Philippines)
•	Bayt al-Imam (Jordan)	•	Al-Ittihad Al Islamiya - AIAI (Somalia)
•	Lashkar-e-Taiba and Jaish-e-Muhammad (Kashmir & India)	•	Islamic Movement of Uzbekistan
•	Asbat al Ansar (Lebanon)	•	Islamic Army of Aden (Yemen)
•	Hezbollah (Lebanon)		Jama'at al-Tawhid wa al- Jihad of Iraq

The aim of the organization is unlikely to undergo a change and will be to remain glued the larger one of establishing a pan Islamic Caliphate, fighting the United States and overthrowing the near enemy or regimes in the Middle East. For coordination of strategies and priorities the al Qaeda uses the instrument of councils or shuras where these facets are debated in detail and a common view obtained. Once there is consensus then all members have to abide by the collective decision.[35]

---

[35] Seth G Jones. The Al Qaeda Thr eat in P akistan. Testimony presented before the House Homeland Security Committee, Subcommittee on Counterterrorism and Intelligence on May 3, 2011. RAND Corporation. Santa Monica. 2011

The Al Qaeda's organization expansion strategy is described by analysts as Daniel Byman in typical modern management jargon as that of, "Mergers and acquisitions". The first major mer ger after 9/1 1 was that of Salafist Group for Preaching and Combat (GSPC by its French initials), on 1   1 September 2006. It was the present chief of the group who made the announcement, " The Salafist Group for Preaching and Combat has joined the Al Qaeda organization," Ayman al-Zawahiri, al Qaeda's then Number 2, stated, "May this be a bone in the throat oAmerican and French crusaders, and their allies, and sow fear in the hearts of French traitors and sons of apostates."

The GSPC soon named itself the (AQIM) and also attempted to go from local to global.Yemen-based al Qaeda in theArabian Peninsula (AQAP) which had recruited the Nigerian youth who had attempted to blow up a passenger airplane landing in Detroit was also a merger of sorts between the jihadists in Yemen and Saudi Arabia in 2009. [36] Zawahiri's Egyptian Islamic Jihad (EIJ) was also the result of just such a merger many years earlier providing the waning image of the group a global profile. The process of merging with the Al Qaeda is said to be long. Zawahiri's group the EIJ was on some sort of a probation for over 10 years while the AQIM waited for almost 4 years before final anointment.[37] Zarqawi's group in Iraq, Jamaat al-Tawhid wal-Jihad and Salafist Group for Preaching and Combat (GSPC) joined the al Qaeda based on the principle of seniority rather than capability as both had larger resources and fighters than the central organization per se. thus the two groups AQ Iraq and AQIM emerged.[38]

---

[36] Daniel Byman. Al Qaeda's M&A Strategy. 7 December 2010. http://www.foreignpolicy.com/articles/2010/12/07/al_qaedas_m_and_a_strategy?print=yes&hidecomments=yes&page=full

[37] Daniel Byman. Al Qaeda's M&A Strategy. 7 December 2010. http://www.foreignpolicy.com/articles/2010/12/07/al_qaedas_m_and_a_strategy?print=yes&hidecomments=yes&page=full

[38] Leah F arrall. How Al Qaeda W orks? Foreign Af fairs. Mar ch/April 2011. ht tp://www.foreignaffairs.com/articles/67467/leah-farrall/how-al-qaeda-works

Those groups which are now aspiring to join the Al Qaeda are Somalia's al-Shabab as "al Qaeda of the Horn of Africa." [39] As Shabab, has not been admitted despite declaration of loyalty to the Al Qaeda because the latter has a relationship with another Somali group Hizbul Islam. However in case the As Shabab carries out an attack successfully in some external area it may be brought under the Al Qaeda umbrella in the future. This may be the only likely organization that may come under the Al Qaeda in the future as others including Jemaah Islamiyah splinter Jamaah Ansharut Tauhid with a small subsidiary "al Qaeda in Aceh," is not likely to want to lose its identity through affiliation with the Al Qaeda. [40]

Normally it is seen that support within such groups for joining the Al Qaeda may not be universal and this can be used to possibly engineer a split. [41] Thus the Al Qaeda has adopted the merger and acquisition as a major form of expanding the organization. The merger and acquisition strategy enables the Al Qaeda to virtually double its reach overnight as well as provides ideological and logistics support in terms of arms and gun running networks, drug linkages and so on. The access that the Al Qaeda gets to expatriate communities in foreign countries is another gain for instance it is said that the large Somali diaspora in the United States will be at the beck and call of the group, if As Shabab joins the Al Qaeda. [42] The Al Qaeda brand image is one of the most important gains for local groups providing it a global profile and expanding influence amongst peers. [43]

---

[39] Daniel Byman. Al Qaeda's M&A Strategy. 7 December 2010. http://www.foreignpolicy.com/articles/2010/12/07/al_qaedas_m_and_a_strategy?print=yes&hidecomments=yes&page=full

[40] Leah Farrall. How Al Qaeda Works? Foreign Affairs. March/April 2011. http://www.foreignaffairs.com/articles/67467/leah-farrall/how-al-qaeda-works

[41] Daniel Byman. Al Qaeda's M&A Strategy. 7 December 2010. http: www.foreignpolicy.com/articles/2010/12/07/al_qaedas_m_and_a_strategy?print= yes&hidecomments=yes&page=full

[42] Daniel Byman. Al Qaeda's M&A Strategy. 7 December 2010. http://www.foreignpolicy.com/rticles/2010/12/07/al_qaedas_m_and_a_strategy?print=yes&hidecomments=yes&page=full

[43] Daniel Byman. Al Qaeda's M&A Strategy. 7 December 2010. http://www.foreignpolicy.com/articles/2010/12/07/al_qaedas_m_and_a_strategy?print=yes&hidecomments=yes&page=full

The Al Qaeda is thus able to provide strategic guidance, encourage major terrorist strikes, conduct training, provide financial assistance and conduct a propaganda campaign to give greater visibility to terrorist activities. In turn all these activities which are self supporting facilitate in expanding the reach of group ideology and networks. If such is the evolved organizational system, it would be evident that the al Qaeda will be able to survive the leadership crisis particularly as it has despite the challenges of leadership selected Zawahiri as its next leader.

How Al Qaeda Functions – theAdaptive Network?

The Al Qaeda is as per Leah Farral, theAustralian counter terrorism expert that of "devolved network." The command structure is flexible between the centre, the branches and the franchises. Seth Jones refers to the Al Qaeda as a, "complex adaptive system," which uses a large number of diverse networks to achieve its aim and adapts from experience[44] The core focuses on strategic command and control. This is exercised not physically but by identifying the types of attacks which can convey the message to the target audience through video releases of acts of terror . The actual conduct and management of the network is left to the branch and franchise heads. The philosophy being that with a*manhaj* there is no need for day to day control of operations.Another role of the central structure is to coordinate operations outside the area of a branch. [45]

The al Qaeda branches are not required to owe allegiance to Osama Bin Laden but the leaders of the franchises have to swear faithfulness to Osama. How will this arrangement work and will Zawahiri be able to attract the same followership as Osama, in particular from leaders of franchises, remains to be seen. These groups may attempt to branch out on their own until a unifying event or a singular push by Zawahiri can bring them together

---

[44] Seth G Jones, The Al Qaeda Thr eat in P akistan. Testimony presented bef ore the House Homeland Security Committee, Subcommittee on Counterterrorism and Intelligence on May 3, 2011. RAND Corporation. Santa Monica. 2011

[45] Leah F arrall. How Al Qaeda W orks? *Foreign Affairs*. Mar ch/April 2011. ht tp:// www.foreignaffairs.com/articles/67467/leah-farrall/how-al-qaeda-works

For legitimacy of terrorAl Qaeda leadership relies on, "takfiri," thought of attacking corrupt regimes on Muslim land and the global enemy United States and the West. Takfiri ideology also calls for unity on the basis of capability of groups or seniority, the Al Qaeda invariably prefers the latter and to that extent is conservative. [46] The al Qaeda strategy is of a "transference policy" wherein each franchise finds its own ways of targeting such as the cargo explosives technique developed in 2010. [47]

There are differences in functioning between local groups and the al Qaeda. The latter encourages international rather than local targets. The Al Qaeda wants to believe that it targets only international regimes and not locals which are left to the affiliates in the region. The aim of the group is to change the orientation from the local to the global thus it prefers to send a similar message through its targeted attacks. [48] There can be exceptions as the AQIM has continued to engage targets in Algeria even though it is now also focusing on France, US and Israel and is destroying economic infrastructure.[49]

Another prominent difference between al Qaeda and the local groups is the use of suicide and car bombs by the former while locals go in for small scale attacks. [50] The category of targets designated by the group such as public transportation, government buildings, and vital infrastructure are standard only large-scale plots or new targets require approval of the central leadership.[51] The decision by the leadership to assign targets outside areas

---

[46] Leah Farrall. How Al Qaeda Works? Foreign Affairs. March/April 2011. ht tp://www.foreignaffairs.com/articles/67467/leah-farrall/how-al-qaeda-works

[47] Mr. Riad Kahwaji, CEO, INEGMA. Dr. Theodore Karasik, Director R&D, INEGMA. May 2011. The Security Implications of Bin Laden's Death.

[48] Daniel Byman. Al Qaeda's M&A Strategy. 7 December 2010. http://www.foreignpolicy.com/articles/2010/12/07/al_qaedas_m_and_a_strategy?printyes& hidecomments=yes&page=full

[49] Daniel Byman. Al Qaeda's M&A Strategy. 7 December 2010. http: www.foreignpolicy.com/articles/2010/12/07al_qaedas_m_and_a_strategy?print= yes&hidecomments=yes&page=full

[50] Daniel Byman. Al Qaeda's M&A Strategy. 7 December 2010. http://www.foreignpolicy.com/articles/2010/12/07/al_qaedas_m_and_a_strategy?print= yes&hidecomments=yes&page=full

[51] Leah Farrall. How Al Qaeda Works? Foreign Affairs. March/April 2011. ht tp://www.foreignaffairs.com/articles/67467/leah-farrall/how-al-qaeda-works

will depend as much on the capability of the group as on the inter group and inter personal relations, the closer the same the more is the likelihood of acceding to these requests. [52]

Zarqawi for instance sought permission to expand operations to Jordan. Similarly when one branch is under pressure the area can be allotted to other branches. The AQAP was delegated responsibility to carry out operations against the US in 2002 when the A Q Central was under pressure[53]

The Al Qaeda – The Network

The Zawahiri Era

As would be evident from the preceding discussion, the al Qaeda today comprises of the al Qaeda Central,   AQAP, AQIM and al-Qaeda in the Land of Two Rivers (Iraq). [54] Al Qaeda offshoots today are spread across the globe including some of the Scandinavian countries as Sweden and Norway. For them Bin Laden was a guide and philosopher   . [55] They are unlikely to however merely wither away after his death. "W e've struck a substantial blow at part of the [radical Islamic] movement, but this is far far from over," said James Woolsey, a former director of the Central Intelligence Agency. [56] The al Qaeda core continues to comprise of leaders who are, "highly skilled, dedicated, well-trained, and meticulous about operational security". [57]

---

[52] Leah F arrall. How Al Qaeda W orks? Foreign Af fairs. Mar ch/April 2011. ht tp:// www.foreignaffairs.com/articles/67467/leah-farrall/how-al-qaeda-works

[53] Leah F arrall. How Al Qaeda W orks? Foreign Af fairs. Mar ch/April 2011. ht tp:// www.foreignaffairs.com/articles/67467/leah-farrall/how-al-qaeda-works

[54] Mr. Riad Kahwaji, CEO, INEGMA. Dr. Theodore Karasik, Director R&D, INEGMA. May 2011. The Security Implications of Bin Laden's Death.

[55] U.S. to Probe Pakistan Support for bin Laden. http://online.wsj.com/article/ SB10001424052748704569404576299500647391240.html

[56] U.S. to Probe Pakistan Support for bin Laden. http://online.wsj.com/article/ SB10001424052748704569404576299500647391240.html

[57] Daniel Byman. Al Qaeda's M&A Strategy. 7 December 2010. http://www.foreignpolicy.com/ articles/2010/12/07al_qaedas_m_and_a_strategy?print=yes&hidecomments=yes& page=full

Ayman Zawahiri, the former Egyptian second in command who is regarded as a strategist and organizer now leads the Group. Egyptian, Saif al-Adel was selected by al-Qaeda's s inner circle to replace bin Laden temporarily but soon Zawahiri took his rightful place. Zawahiri's elevation to the number one post in al-Qaeda was anticipated after he had sang and eulogy in the praise of Bin Laden and also pledged allegiance of the Al Qaeda to Quetta Shura Taliban. It is said that only the head of the al Qaeda could assure Mullah Omar and be accepted by him. [58] His book, "*Knights Under the Prophet's Banner*," outlines his philosophy and he has succeeded Osama one and half months after his death.

He has been seen as a philosopher-guide and al Qaeda operational commanders have been far more active and leading the charge so to say of the organisation as Abu Musab al Zarqawi in Iraq to Anwar al-Awlaki in Yemen. [59] Saif al-Din al Ansari al Adel, the organisations present 'military commander', Amin al Haq Afghan, the 'security coordinator' and Suleiman Abu Ghaith, al Qaeda's spokesman are as per noted Indian counter terrorism expert Ajai Sahni some other prominent Al Qaeda leaders. The Al Qaeda has possibly gone in for seniority instead of operational capability or charisma. [60]

Zawahiri also believes in mass casualty terrorist attacks and establish a base in a nation with a view to expand from there in other areas. [61] For Zawahiri the main challenge would be to rejuvenate the organization and see that the loss of information from the raid on Bin Laden's compound is limited. This may lead to a level of dissonance in the Al Qaeda which has to be exploited by a relentless offensive against the leadership. [62]

---

[58] William McCants. The Zawahiri Era Begins. http://afpak.foreignpolicy.com/posts/2011/06/16/the_zawahiri_era_begins

[59] U.S. to Probe Pakistan Support for bin Laden. http://online.wsj.com/article/SB10001424052748704569404576299500647391240.html

[60] Mr. Riad Kahwaji, CEO, INEGMA. Dr. Theodore Karasik, Director R&D, INEGMA. May 2011. The Security Implications of Bin Laden's Death.

[61] Mr. Riad Kahwaji, CEO, INEGMA. Dr. Theodore Karasik, Director R&D, INEGMA. May 2011. The Security Implications of Bin Laden's Death.

[62] Brynjar Lia. Al Qaeda Without Bin Laden. How Terrorists Cope With their Leader's Death. http://www.foreignaffairs.com/articles/67846/brynjar-lia/al-qaeda-without-bin-laden

Zawahiri's first challenge is to survive for the Americans egged by the success of Bin Laden's assassination are likely to be hot on the trail of the Number 1 leader now if not already having made some success in tracking him. Thus he would be ensuring that the trail which could also lead from Bin Laden's document trove is obliterated. Zawahiri would have also to get the factions together which is always a challenge for a group which functions more on inspirational leadership and mentoring which requires a strong personality. Moreover as an Egyptian, Zawahiri will always be suspect in the eyes of the Arabs of the al Qaeda who are essentially been the mainstay of the organization. [63]

The initial reactions from the United States after news of nomination of Zawahiri as the Al Qaeda Chief filtered in were less than flattering. In a routine daily conference on 16 June White House Press Secretary Jay Carney when asked for his reaction on Zawahiri taking the lead of Al Qaeda remarked, "Certainly not surprising. He was identified prior to the successful mission against Osama bin Laden as al Qaeda's number two. It's neither surprising nor does it change some fundamental facts, which is al Qaeda's ideology is bankrupt. The fact is that peaceful movements for change are the future of the region and al Qaeda is the past. That was true before Osama bin Laden's death and is true today". [64]

John Brennan the US President Barack Obama's top counter terrorism adviser was even more disdainful on Zawahiri. In the post mission Conference he had remarked that, "The number two, Zawahiri is not charismatic. He has not been — was not involved in the fight earlier on in Afghanistan... and I think he has a lot of detractors within the organization. And I think you're going to see them start eating themselves from within more and more." Brennan reportedly released some additional talking points to the media after nomination of Zawahiri as the leader These depicted Zawahiri as lacking talent for leadership, having no combat

---

[63] William McCants. The Zawahiri Era Begins. http://afpak.foreignpolicy.com/posts/2011/06/16/the_zawahiri_era_begins

[64] June 16, 2011 Pr ess Briefing by Press Secretary Jay Carney, 6/16/2011. ht tp://www.whitehouse.gov/briefing-room/press-briefings

experience, a soft image and in general, "nowhere near the credentials that Osama bin Laden had". [65]

Past experience on terrorist leaders denotes that it is always dangerous to under estimate them for they have the resources and political skills to cause much pain to liberal, post modern democracies as the United States. More over of the two main strands of leadership in terrorist organizations, strategic ideologues and operational, Zawahiri belongs to the more dangerous former one. Thus some restraint would have been advisable but perhaps this was a part of the larger strategic communication campaign by the Americans against the Al Qaeda.

Zawahiri thus has his task cut out to emerge out of the Bin Laden shadow. He will also have to ensure that he is able to retain support of strong allies as the Taliban and the pledge he made in his first speech was possibly directed towards winning such an assurance as well as indicating to others that the two groups were together despite the demise of Bin Laden. Then there are ongoing battles in Yemen, where Zawahiri may have much lesser influence than Bin Laden who was a native from that country with filial linkages including that of his youngest wife who hailed from there. The situation in Yemen may be his first test and thus will be a key challenge that he would have to meet in the days ahead. [66]

Nevertheless Zawahiri is a formidable and experienced terrorist leader who has the skills to lead the Al Qaeda and the seniority to go along with it, but for an organization which has survived on Bin Laden's charisma how much will the bespectacled Egyptian doctor be able to inspire remains to be seen. [67]

As per Leah Farral, Australian expert on counter terrorism the delay in announcing the leadership of Zawahiri is attributed more to the security

---

[65] Josh Rogin . White House: Zawahiri is an "armchair general" and "soft" Foreign Policy Blog.

[66] William McCants. The Zawahiri Era Begins. http://afpak.foreignpolicy.com/posts/2011/06/16/the_zawahiri_era_begins

[67] William McCants. The Zawahiri Era Begins. http://afpak.foreignpolicy.com/posts/2011/06/16/the_zawahiri_era_begins

arrangements for the shura to confer and confirm rather than any infighting, thus there were clearly no leadership challenges to him on the horizon. This would have also followed a reorganization of the command of the group with the hierarchy down the ladder and principally how contact will be maintained with the new leader, given that the manual courier system also seems to be penetrable. Throwing away the current trail was also important therefore this would have also taken some tie. There will be also question of nominating a deputy and this is likely to come about shortly.[68] It is believed that the council members followed the rules while nominating   Ayman al Zawahiri as the successor to Bin Laden.

Another challenge for Zawahiri is to find the funding which Bin Laden could tap through his contacts amongst the Saudi financers of Al Qaeda. Zawahiri an Egyptian may face some challenges in which case again the group's potential and the Al Qaeda's leaders own credibility will be questioned.[69] The communication with the younger leadership may also pose a problem for Zawahiri who is known to be an old conservative.[70] To keep in touch with the younger leaders and   Western oriented youth increasingly joining the al Qaeda, Adam Gadahn, also known as Azzam the American, formerly of Orange County California is likely to gain prominence as an assistant to Zawahiri as per J.M. Berger editor of Intelwire.com and author of the new book, Jihad Joe: Americans Who Go to War in the Name of Islam.[71]

Al Qaeda Central

The al Qaeda central is based in the tribal areas of   Af-Pak. Zawahiri is likely to be based in the same region. Interestingly as per Bill Roggio, the l

---

[68] Leah Farrall. The Zawahiri Era Begins. http://afpak.foreignpolicy.com/posts/2011/06/16/the_zawahiri_era_begins

[69] Daveed Gartenstein-Ross. The Zawahiri Era Begins. http://afpak.foreignpolicy.com/posts/2011/06/16/the_zawahiri_era_begins

[70] Daveed Gartenstein-Ross. The Zawahiri Era Begins. http://afpak.foreignpolicy.com/posts/2011/06/16/the_zawahiri_era_begins

[71] J.M. Berger. The Zawahiri Era Begins. http://afpak.foreignpolicy.com/posts/2011/06/16/the_zawahiri_era_begins

Qaeda has appointed the current leader of the allied Turkistan Islamic Party to command al Qaeda forces in Pakistan and organize training camps there before Osama bin Laden was killed. Roggio claims that Abdul Shakoor Turkistani, the chief of the Turkistan Islamic Party is in command in Federally Administered Tribal Areas (FATA) after Saif al Adel left the region. He quotes this based on information from Karachi Islam associated with the Al Rashid Trust, a charity which also acts as an al Qaeda front. [72] Does this nomination denote the aim of spreading the insurgency in China's Xinjiang province by giving importance to a prominent leader from the area?

The Turkic Islamic Party is reported to be having a base in the Mir Ali region of North Waziristan. Abdul Shakoor would have possibly won approval due to his cordial relations with key top Taliban leaders Hafiz Gul Bahadar Mullah Nazir and Hakeemullah Mehsud. Nazir and Gul Bahadur are in a pact with the Pakistan Army and are known to support the same against anti government Taliban mainly from the Mehsud tribe. Importantly the Turkistan Islamic Party and IJU comprising of a break away faction of the more commonly known IMU is reportedly located in Mir Ali and is referred to as the, 'European Taliban,' as Turks and European Muslims have a strong base within. [73] The Turkestan groups have been holding an influential position in the Al Qaeda hierarchy over a period and have a good linkage with all the affiliates, including the Pakistani Taliban and the Haqqani group. Joint meetings are reportedly held between these leaders from time to time in the tribal areas to plan strategy. [74]

As Shakoor will be most certainly a part of the Shura Majlis of the Taliban the aims and objectives of proliferation in Xinjiang and Central Asia

---

[72] Bill Roggio. Al Qaeda appoints new leader of forces in Pakistan's tribal areas. May 9, 2011. http://www.longwarjournal.org/archives/2011/05/al_qaeda_appoints_ne_2.php#ixzz1MEyteihc

[73] Bill Roggio. Al Qaeda appoints new leader of forces in Pakistan's tribal areas. May 9, 2011. http://www.longwarjournal.org/archives/2011/05/al_qaeda_appoints_ne_2.php#ixzz1MEyteihc

[74] Bill Roggio. Al Qaeda appoints new leader of forces in Pakistan's tribal areas. May 9, 2011. http://www.longwarjournal.org/archives/2011/05/al_qaeda_appoints_ne_2.php#ixzz1MEyteihc

should be evident. The Shura Majlis is linked not just as a conglomerate of the top leadership organizationally but through kinship networks and inter marriages. Many of the elite build a strong affinity which is peculiar to these terrorist groups. On the whole though due to large number of leaders and cadres killed in drone attacks al Qaeda Central remains some what marginalized though it is capable of carrying out high profile terrorist attacks as that on Pakistan's base in Karachi, PNS Mehran.

AQAP, AQIM and Others

Al Qaeda in the Arabian Peninsula, or AQAP is led by Nasir al Wahishi. Wahishi is a Bin Laden proximate who escaped to Iran from Afghanistan, was arrested, extradited toYemen in 2003, escaped from prison in 2006 and formed AQAP in 2009.[75] Wahishi is known as kunya. He has brought about resurgence in the operations there.

A Saudi named Ibrahim Suleiman al-Rubaish is the main AQAP ideologue. Al Awlaki of AQAP is possibly better known due to the *Inspire* magazine series he launched and is the propaganda head. Al-Awlaki and al-Rubaish are supported by, Adel bin Abdullah al-Abab, a Yemeni imam who reportedly chairs AQAP's Shariah Council.[76] Al Awalaki lacks formal education in Islamic interpretation but assists t others in spreading the message more ef fectively in English. al-A wlaki has thus emer ged as an important ideologue and spokesman for especially to English-speaking Muslims.[77] He is not a good guerrilla organizer but is in fact only an effective communicator who has been a regular contributor to the English-language *Inspire* magazine. The *Inspire* gives a justification in one of the issues for attacks on those who have drawn the Danish cartoons, thereby providing motivation to others who are inclined to launch lone ranger attacks.

With trouble brewing in Yemen after the fall of President Saleh who had to be evacuated to Saudi Arabia after an attack on his palace in

---

[75] Osama Bin Laden Is Dead. http://online.wsj.com/article/SB10001424052748703 703304576299041912668436.html

[76] Al Qaeda's Leadership in Yemen By Scott Stewart.

[77] Ibid.

Sanaa, the AQAP will play a major role and may gain a strategic hold thereby possibility of Al Qaeda centre of gravity shifting from Af Pak to Yemen remains strong. [78] The deposed Yemeni President Saleh will likely use Bin Laden's death as an excuse to return to power because he will argue that he needs to remain in charge to help squash any attempts by AQAP from gaining more ground and expanding operations. [79]

AQAP has targeted the United States with the foiled plot to bomb cargo planes in October 2010 and at present appears to be the strongest with the leadership, ideology, training, and media capabilities.

Abu Musab Abdel Wadoud, the leader of AQIM is having a hold over operations in Algeria, Mauritania and other parts of Western Africa. [80] The Al Qaeda in Maghreb has been involved in failed airline attack involving, Mr. Abdulmutallab a Nigerian, and three suicide bombings in July 2010 at restaurants in the Ugandan capital, Kampala, as patrons watched the World Cup soccer tournament. [81] AQIM, has also been linked to several killings and kidnappings of Westerners. [82] Presently it is holding French hostages and is seen to be operationally very dangerous but lacks the depth of AQAP.

AQIM has not attacked outside its region, but al Qaeda in Iraq (AQI) was reportedly involved in the June 2007 London and Glasgow bomb plots. [83] The AQI is marginalized now but has suficient capability to keep the interests of the organization in Iraq alive.

---

[78] Osama Bin Laden Is Dead. http://online.wsj.com/article/SB1000142405274870 3703304576299041912668436.html

[79] Mr. Riad Kahwaji, CEO, INEGMA. Dr. Theodore Karasik, Director R&D, INEGMA. May 2011. The Security Implications of Bin Laden's Death.

[80] Mr. Riad Kahwaji, CEO, INEGMA. Dr. Theodore Karasik, Director R&D, INEGMA. May 2011. The Security Implications of Bin Laden's Death.

[81] Osama Bin Laden Is Dead. http://online.wsj.com/article/SB1000142405274 8703703304576299041912668436.html

[82] Osama Bin Laden Is Dead. http://online.wsj.com/article/SB100014240527487037 033045762990419126688436.html

[83] Leah Farrall. How Al Qaeda Works? Foreign Affairs. March/April 2011. ht tp:// www.foreignaffairs.com/articles/67467/leah-farrall/how-al-qaeda-works

The New Look Al Qaeda

While strengthening its legacy and strategic core, the al Qaeda is putting into place a strategy that will make it attractive to deviant Muslim youth in the West. It has already launched two glossy magazines in English, *Inspire* and *The Majestic Woman*. The originator of, "*Inspire*," is said to be Samir Khan. He wanted to create a paper which could appeal to Muslim youth and thus evolved an attractive, "in-flight," type of format. The content was however extremist as is seen from some of the articles of the Summer 2010 edition which were entitled, "Make A Bomb In The Kitchen Of Your Mom," "The Way To Save The Earth-A Message From Shaykh Usamah Bin Ladin," "Sending & Receiving Encrypted Messages." The Toner bomb that could be transported through toners for print cartridges was featured in the November 2010 edition on the front page. The total cost of this bomb was highlighted as, " 4,200." [84] This was a clear message to the youth, you can make a bomb in the basement at low cost.

The version for women, again a glossy was named as, *Al-Shamikha*, or "*The Majestic Woman*." Here a women with a niqab is posed with a submachine gun on the cover but includes feminine tips on the lines of Cosmopolitan or Elle. [85] Al – Shamika shrewdly propagates Niqab to preserve facial complexion from rays of the Sun while eulogizing the lives of wives of martyrs. While the actual impact of these tabloids is not clear so far, they are establishing a dangerous trend which has to be examined in greater detail.

Online presence of the Al Qaeda has provided it a unique forum to inspire and motivate cadres globally and gain their support. The internet also is used as a medium to provide self help kits for making bombs and IEDS or directing lone wolf attacks as by Major Nidal which can create

---

[84] James Veitch and John Martin, *The Death of Osama Bin Laden and the Future of Al Qaeda* Bangladesh Institute of Peace and Security Studies. Dhaka 2011.

[85] James Veitch and John Martin, *The Death of Osama Bin Laden and the Future of Al Qaeda* Bangladesh Institute of Peace and Security Studies. Dhaka 2011.

enough stresses not just in local communities but also internationally[86]

This has led some analysts to believe that the   Al Qaeda may be diversifying its tactics from catastrophic mass casualty attacks to that of a," thousand cuts," again highlighted in the Inspire magazine in November 2010. This strategy of large number of small terror attacks may be used by the organization in the phase of regrouping after Bin Laden, but their impact is generally local and if this is the trade mark that emerges for the group, it will lose much of its aura that was reflected in 9/11 and the many mass attacks that followed.[87]

The new strategy also implies that recruits need not come to Pakistan for training nor seek permission or instructions for launching terrorist attacks. They can do so on their own.   [88] This is a new breed of, "lone rangers," estranged youth having a grouse against society in which they live and radicalized enough to give up their life to seek a change.   The, "*Inspire,*" magazine shows them the so called, "light," at the end of what they see a dark tunnel in a modern society.

Maj. Nidal Hasan, who went on a shooting spree at Fort Hood in Texas in 2009, and Umar Farouk   Abdulmutallab, the underwear bomber who attempted to blow up a U.S. bound passenger plane on Christmas Day the same year are part of this new breed of al Qaeda fighters who have no direct link with the central organization but their acts are clearly attributed to some of the motivations by AQAP leader Awlaki. [89] Anwar al-Awlaki is suspected to have directed Major Nidal Hasan to carry out a terrorist attack at Fort Hood in the United States in 2009. [90]

---

[86] Shir az Maher . I slamist W eb Sites and The Future of Al Qaeda. http:// www.foreignaffairs.com/articles/67841/shiraz-maher/jihadis-react-to-bin-ladens-death

[87] Daveed Gartenstein-Ross. The Zawahiri Era Begins. http://afpak.foreignpolicy.com/posts/ 2011/06/16/the_zawahiri_era_begins

[88] Osama Bin Laden Is Dead. http://online.wsj.com/article/SB10001424052748703703 304576299041912668436.html

[89] Osama Bin Laden Is Dead. http://online.wsj.com/article/SB1000142405274870 37033045762299041912668436.html

[90] Shir az Maher . I slamist W eb Sites and The Future of Al Qaeda. http:// www.foreignaffairs.com/articles/67841/shiraz-maher/jihadis-react-to-bin-ladens-death

The lone wolf attacks are also the main feature of the 100-minute video featuring Adam Gadahn and Abu Yahya al-Libi praising Fort Hood shooter Nidal Malik Hasan, Dutch filmmaker   Theo van Gogh's killer Mohammed Bouyeri, and fundamentalist Rabbi Meir Kahanes assassin El-Sayyid Nosair. This is no doubt a change from the overall strategy of the group to go for major targets. On the other hand this could be also seen as a supplicant strategy to eliminate the local resistors supporting the main one.[91] In October 2010, Gadahn was the one who released a statement refuting the Mardin Conference, a March 2010 effort by mainstream Muslim clerics to undercut al-Qaeda's key theological underpinnings.[92]

The potential of these lone rangers may however be limited but this will place an unprecedented pressure on the already hard pressed intelligence agencies across the World to trace and track a lar ge number of deviant youth who are spread across the world.

Seth Jones of the Rand Corporation in a Testimony to the Congress Foreign Affairs Committee on 24 May 2011 after the assassination of bin Laden summarizes the threat thus, "Al Qaeda and allied groups continue to present a grave threat to the United States and its allies overseas by overseeing and encouraging terrorist operations, managing a robust propaganda campaign, conducting training, and collecting and distributing financial assistance".[93] Organizationally the group's branches apart from Al Qaeda Central such as the AQAP, AQIM and affiliates as the Tehrik-e-Taliban Pakistan (Pakistan), Lashkare-Tayyiba (Pakistan), and al Shabaab (Somalia) posed threat of terrorist attacks in the US homeland as per Seth.[94] Stephen Tankel, from the Carnegie Endowment for International Peace told in a Senate hearing that the Lashkar eTaiyyaba (LeT) could well plot a

---

[91] Da veed Gartenstein-R oss. ht tp://www.foreignpolicy.com/articles/2011/06/16/ the_zawahiri_era_begins?page=0,2

[92] J.M. Berger. http://afpak.foreignpolicy.com/posts/2011/06/16/the_zawahiri_era_begins

[93] Seth G Jones. The Future of Al Qaeda. May 2011. Testimony presented before the House Foreign Aff airs Commit tee, Subcommi ttee on T errorism, Nonpro liferation and T rade on May 24, 2011. RAND Corporation. Santa Monica. 2011.

[94] Seth G Jones. The Future of Al Qaeda. May 2011. Testimony presented before the House Foreign Aff airs Commit tee, Subcommi ttee on T errorism, Nonpro liferation and T rade on May 24, 2011. RAND Corporation. Santa Monica. 2011.

larger and wider terrorist attack after bin Laden' s death, "LeT' s position remains relatively secure in Pakistan". [95] The overall challenge therefore remains formidable.

A critical dimension of theAl Qaeda is likelihood of the group attaining capability of conducting a mass terror attack using Nuclear , Biological, Chemical (NBC) or radiological means. This neatly fits in with the ability of the group to think and operate strategically and its main USP of mass casualty high visibility terror attacks.After 9/11 it has also been seeking dirty bombs. A report in the LosAngeles Times by Greg Miller highlighted contact with Sultan Bashirrudin Mahmood and Chaudhry Abdul Majeed two Pakistani nuclear experts who had met Osama Bin Laden in 2001. [96] The Al Qaeda had also followed up anthrax attacks after the strikes in New York in September and October 2001. NBC or radiological capability will provide the group an inflection to rise up from the shock of demise of Bin Laden, thus intelligence agencies across the World would have to focus on this dangerous challenge in the days ahead.

Ending Al Qaeda – Some Thoughts

An overview of theAl Qaeda provided above indicates a number of lessons for targeting the group in the future. The best way to meet the Al-Qaeda challenge in the short term appears to be to focus on the leadership. A series of attacks in rapid succession on top leaders will most certainly cripple the group. However this is not likely to be easy even though theAmericans are most probably following the al Qaeda command chain in tandem. [97] Intelligence led operations against the leadership thus remains the key despite the difficult of targeting an elusive enemy with ample resources. [98]

---

[95] Le T may replace al-Qaeda as terror umbr ella outfi t: US experts http://www.indianexpress.com/news/let-may-replace-alqaeda-as-terror-umbrella-outfit-us-experts/785750/0

[96] Miller, Greg. LA Times Report. 09 November 2007. Available at www.latimes.com/.../la-fg-nukes8nov08,1,3301346.story?coll=la-headlines-world&ctrack=1&cset=true

[97] Leah F arrall. The Z awahiri Era Begins. http://afpak.foreignpolicy.com/posts/2011/06/16/the_zawahiri_era_begins

[98] Mr. Riad Kahwaji, CEO, INEGMA. Dr. Theodore Karasik, Director R&D, INEGMA. May 2011. The Security Implications of Bin Laden's Death.

In the long term, "war," against the al Qaeda or other groups may not be the right strategy . Even after 9/1 1 there were reports that a Pashtun loya jirga in Kandahar, the base of theTaliban was demanding Mullah Omar expel bin Laden andArabs.[99] Similarly there was a huge outcry for bringing down the al Qaeda in NorthernAfghanistan after Ahmad Shah Masood had been killed in a suicide attack by two persons from the group just two days before 9/11. [100] Some analysts feel that mobilising this opposition to Bin Laden and the al Qaeda would have been a far smarter strategy than dropping Special Forces in the country . While this is past history learning lessons from the same may show us the way ahead, as it appears rousing the Muslim masses against ghastly deeds ofAl Qaeda, Taliban and other groups seems to be a better strategy than confronting them upfront.

The al Qaeda will wither only when the support for it dries up. This can happen when the people are turned against it which in turn is possible if perceived sense of persecution in a large section of Islamic population particularly in West Asia and the Af Pak is removed and they are assured that they will get equal if not full rights in the overall balance of global and regional power.

Elimination of cells of theAl Qaeda and other groups which are coercing the population is another dimension of the same challenge. But such groups which rely on the ideology of martyrdom, death is not very fearsome, but refutation of ideology remains a key challenge and thus they are likely to respond far more aggressively to any new interpretations emerging such as the New Mardin Declaration. [101]

Max Boot, noted author and security expert has indicated that the Al Qaeda's demise may not be linked to that of its leader Osama forAl Qaeda resembles more like the Hamas or the Hezbollah which did not perish after its leader was killed. Giving the example of how terrorist groups and

---

[99] Al-Qaeda is not dead http://www.thehindu.com/todays-paper/tp-opinion/article1989672.ece

[100] Al-Qaeda is not dead http://www.thehindu.com/todays-paper/tp-opinion/article1989672.ece

[101] Al Qaeda's Leadership in Yemen By Scott Stewart

insurgencies end, Boot says two groups which collapsed with the removal of the leader were the Shining Path (*Sendero Luminoso*) and the Kurdistan Workers' Party (PKK) — The Shining Path finished with the successful apprehension and incarceration of its leader Abimael Guzmán in 1992 and so did the PKK with the arrest of its leader Abdullah Öcalan in 1999 by Turkey. Both these groups do exist on the ground but lack past strength. This is as per Boot primarily because there was a cult image of these leaders and their arrest was also part of a large counter insurgency campaign undertaken by the respective states against the organizations as a whole.

On the other hand Hamas and Hezbollah, continue to flourish despite the elimination of their leader Sheikh Ahmed Yassin by Israel in 2004 and also his successor, Abdel Aziz Rantisi. Hezbollah's secretary-general, Abbas Mussawi was similarly eliminated by helicopter strike in 1992 while Imad Mughniyeh the operational director in a car bomb attack in 2008. Hamas and the Hezbollah seem to have gone from strength to strength despite the elimination of their leaders thereby indicating the limitations of the decapacitation strategy. [102] Collective leadership and territorial control seems to determine the reason for progression of the Hamas and Hezbollah who also have not faced the type of comprehensive campaign of counter militancy that the PKK or the Shining Path were subjected to. [103]

Boot seems to suggest that leadership decapacitation is only a part of the overall strategy. He states, "In the final analysis, targeting the leadership of an insurgent group is important but not sufficient. Defeating a terrorist or guerrilla organization requires a comprehensive approach that provides ground-level security and basic governance to prevent a shadow regime from taking root. That was the approach taken by the United States in Iraq and now in Afghanistan". Unless the United States or the global coalition is able to commit forces on the ground for territorial control of tribal areas of

---

[102] Max Boot. Al Qaeda's Prognosis. Can Terrorist Groups Live Without Their Leaders? http://www.foreignaffairs.com/articles/67832/max-boot/al-qaedas-prognosis

[103] Max Boot. Al Qaeda's Prognosis. Can Terrorist Groups Live Without Their Leaders? http://www.foreignaffairs.com/articles/67832/max-boot/al-qaedas-prognosis

Pakistan, Yemen, Somalia and others where   Al Qaeda and its af filiates flourish there is unlikely to be any relief from these groups as per Boot.[104]

Thus it would be evident that where a State has gained territorial control and adopted a comprehensive strategy targeting the terrorist groups as well as people at large, there is likely to be some reprieve from terrorism, where there is a general lack of the same, the groups are likely to continue to pose danger to societies and states.

Given the organizational structure of the al Qaeda based on a network of branches, affiliates and others, the aim for counter terrorists should be to separate the Al Qaeda core from the afiliates thereby reducing the influence of the organization and then gradually work towards the central leadership[105]

Keeping more groups from joining the Al Qaeda is also one part of the same strategy. These organizations may be indoctrinated to understand that they may become locally less relevant thus losing out on what has been achieved by groups as the Hamas and Hezbollah who have now an important stake in their respective governments because they preferred to remain local rather than go in for the hyper reality of a pan Islamic caliphate.[106] It is easier to target groups with a nationalist rather than a religious motivation that are not likely to be attracted to the   Al Qaeda. Thus the Hizb ul Mujahideen in Jammu and Kashmir remained away and even resisted presence of Bin Laden's fighters even though insurgency was at its peak in the state in 1990's. [107] These local differences can be very effectively used

---

[104] Max Boot. Al Qaeda's Prognosis. Can Terrorist Groups Live Without Their Leaders? http:/ /www.foreignaffairs.com/articles/67832/max-boot/al-qaedas-prognosis

[105] Daniel Byman. Al Qaedas M&A Strategy. 7 December 2010. http://wwwforeignpolicy.com/ articles/2010/12/07/al_qaedas_m_and_a_strategy?print=yes&hidecomments= yes&page=full

[106] Daniel Byman. Al Qaedas M&A Strategy. 7 December 2010. http://wwwforeignpolicy.com/ articles/2010/12/07/al_qaedas_m_and_a_strategy?print= yes&hidecomments=yes&page=full

[107] Daniel Byman. Al Qaedas M&A Strategy. 7 December 2010. http://wwwforeignpolicy.com/ articles/2010/12/07/al_qaedas_m_and_a_strategy?print= yes&hidecomments= yes&page=full

to split the groups, highlight their atrocities to advantage and gain a moral and media advantage. [108]

From another perspective, Richard A. Falkenrath, Senior Fellow for Counterterrorism and Homeland Security at the Council on Foreign Relations cites political challenges faced in a counter terrorism programme given roots of the same in socio political conflict and the human element. This has a strong co-relationship with how people will perceive the rightness of the government or the guerrilla campaigns. For instance collateral damage, long incarceration and trials, interrogations and recruitment of agents create unusual apprehensions and suspicions amongst local populace thereby their reactions could be unpredictable and have the opposite effect of what the counter terrorism campaigners would like to achieve. [109]

---

[108] Daniel Byman. Al Qaedas M&A Strategy. 7 December 2010. http://wwwforeignpolicy.com/articles/2010/12/07/al_qaedas_m_and_a_strategy?print=yes&hidecomments=yes&page=full

[109] Richard A. Falkenrath. Was Bin Laden the Easy Part? http://www.foreignaffairs.com/articles/67831/richard-a-falkenrath/was-bin-laden-the-easy-part

Containing the Fall Out in South Asia

This Chapter examines the fall out of Bin Laden' s killing in South Asia with particular reference to the backlash in Pakistan, reaction by the Taliban, the situation in   Afghanistan, US Pakistan r elations and the importance of counter terrorism cooperation with Pakistan.

Introduction

The death of Osama Bin Laden in Abbottabad posed a major challenge to the United States, that of containing the adverse reactions in Pakistan and militant retribution inAfghanistan. There are many dimensions to this problem, firstly the discovery of Bin Laden in Abbottabad, a cantonment town very close to the capital raised doubts whether he was under protective custody of the Inter Services Intelligence (ISI), if not then how come the agency one of the most efficient and effective failed to track him. Secondly, issues of violation of sovereignty of the country by the US launching raid without the knowledge of Pakistani government or the armed forces was raised in Islamabad. Thirdly, the inability of the armed forces to detect the raid in time and intercept what was an intrusion raised questions over efficiency and effectiveness of the armed forces. Finally following the backlash of the Taliban and theAl Qaeda particularly after attack on a Pakistani naval base PNS Mehran in Karachi in which two P 3 C Orion maritime reconnaissance aircraft were destroyed by the terrorists the security processes of the armed forces, their penetration by extremists and consequentially the safety and security of Pakistan's nuclear weapons also came up for scrutiny.

Matters came to a head when the opposition leader and former Prime Minister and head of the Pakistan Muslim League Nawaz, Mr Nawaz Sharif and his Party launched a broad side on the armed forces during the budget session in the National   Assembly in June questioning the legitimacy of extensive budgetary allotments to the establishment despite penurious state of the economy. Nawaz Sharif who was exiled by former army chief and President Pervez Musharraf from the country after a 1999 coup has had very strained relations with theArmy over a period.The Army in turn lashed back at political leaders as Sharif through the medium of the Corps Commanders Conference. Thus the tit for tat has continued ever since.

The Al Qaeda ever alert to exploit an opportunity to widen the breach between two states called upon the people of Pakistan to rise up. US Monitoring Group SITE intelligence reported an Al Qaeda statement on 6 May exhorting the Pakistani people to rebel. "W e call upon our Muslim people in Pakistan, on whose land Sheikh Osama was killed, to rise up and revolt to cleanse this shame that has been attached to them by a clique of traitors and thieves who sold everything to the enemies.We call upon them to rise up strongly and in general to cleanse their country (Pakistan) from the filth of the Americans who spread corruption in it," said the statement. [1] Newly anointed Al Qaeda Chief in his first statement in the 28-minute video, titled "The Noble Knight Dismounted," also exhorted Pakistanis to rise up against their leaders, "just as your brothers inTunisia, Egypt, Libya and Syria have done." [2]

Underlying these tensions however is the larger global challenge of containing the instability in the Afghanistan Pakistan cauldron which has provided a safe sanctuary for the Al Qaeda amongst other terrorist groups. The International SecurityAssistance Force (ISAF) led by the NorthAtlantic Treaty Organisation (NATO) is involved in an intense counter insurgency campaign in Afghanistan, whose base is mainly in the tribal areas of Pakistan

---

[1] Al Qaeda confirms Osama bin Laden's death. Available at http://www.dawn.com/2011/05/06/al-qaeda-confirms-osama-bin-ladens-death.html

[2] Al Qaeda confirms Osama bin Laden's death. Available at http://www.dawn.com/2011/05/06/al-qaeda-confirms-osama-bin-ladens-death.html

particularly in North Waziristan. It is imperative that the Pakistani Army launches operations to clear this area which is now considered the black hole of international terrorism. For this intelligence and operational cooperation between Pakistan and the United States is necessary, sadly this has virtually broken down after 2 May 2011, with Islamabad restricting deployment of CIA operatives in the county as well as asking US as well as UK military trainers to pull out. Yet Pakistan will remain one of the key factors to contain the growth of the Al Qaeda and the general campaign against terror.

Concerns on theAfghan front also arise as US President Barack Obama announced pull out of troops from the country starting end 2011 and extending up to 2014. His military commanders called this as too, "aggressive". This has set off a chain reaction with other countries announcing a similar draw down of forces in the coming years, even as the Taliban continue to retain sufficient capability to cause incessant violence in the countryTherefore a detailed review of the nuances of the Af Pak situation consequent to the death of Osama Bin Laden are reflected upon in the succeeding paragraphs.

Reactions in Pakistan and Fall Out

The assassination of Osama Bin Laden on 2 May 2011 was as has been mentioned earlier traumatic for the government, the military, the political parties, civil society as well as the public at large in Pakistan. The Tehreek e Taliban which owes allegiance to the al Qaeda was quick to launch reprisal attacks leading to further pain for the Army and the intelligence agencies demonstrating their failure to meet the challenge.

First of all and most importantly the ordinary Pakistani was confused, outraged as well as embarrassed by the Bin Laden killing in their backyard. Three in ten Pakistanis believed that the ISI knew of the presence of Bin Laden in Abbottabad. [3]Some openly questioned the status of their country as US expert on Pakistan C Christine Fair records, "We are either a rogue

---

[3] C. Christine F air. Try to see it my wa y. http://afpak.foreignpolicy.com/posts/2011/05/24/
try_to_see_it_my_way

state or a failed state."[4]The civil society particularly Human RightsActivist as Ashma Jahangir came out openly against theArmy. "Previously, security matters in Pakistan were considered very holy, too sacred to be dictated," said Ahsan Iqbal, a senior figure in opposition leader Nawaz Sharifs party reflected. "Now people are asking questions." [5]

Najam Sethi editor of FridayTimes stated that the "angry or confused," Pakistani public is asking tough questions from the Pakistani military high command, "Why wasn't the Pak security establishment able to detect and stop an American incursion into its sovereign space? How come Osama was in a safe compound in the militarys̈ backyard, especially since another terrorist, Omer Patek, an Indonesian, was flushed out from   Abbottabad only two months ago in a joint ISI-CIA operation? What will the military do in the event of another boots-on-ground US operation in Pakistan, either in Waziristan or in any urban area of Pakistan that violates Pakistani sovereignty? Will there be any accountability of those who are responsible for one of the most embarrassing and problematic moments in Pakistan' s history?"[6]

The anger within the services was also palpable as General   Ashfaq Kayani, personally held meetings at three bases within a month where he faced queries from many disgruntled of ficers who questioned American betrayal. A diplomat remarked that the General was getting a lot of flak, "he's getting a rough ride inside the military" He added: "I dont think he's in a comfortable place." [7]

Politically the leader of the parliamentary opposition demanded that President Asif Ali Zardari and Prime Minister Yousaf Raza Gilani resign. "The operation tramples on our honour and dignity, and the president and prime minister must either give an explanation or resign," Chaudhry Nisar

[4] C. Christine F air. Try to see it my wa y. http://afpak.foreignpolicy.com/posts/2011/05/24/try_to_see_it_my_way

[5] http://www.guardian.co.uk/world/2011/jun/01/pakistan-osama-bin-laden-military

[6] Najam Sethi. Operation Get OBL. Available at http://www.thefridaytimes.com/06052011/page1.shtml

[7] http://www.guardian.co.uk/world/2011/jun/01/pakistan-osama-bin-laden-military

Ali told reporters. "The government is keeping silent and there appears to be nobody to respond to propaganda against Pakistan," he added, saying that people in the country were feeling "insecure" after the covert US mission. "Those who are responsible must admit and quit," said Nisar. He also criticised the Inter-Services Intelligence (ISI), saying that Pakistani institutions had "deviated from their real role". Opposition leader Imran Khan and former foreign minister Shah Mehmood Qureshi who are seen to be strong detractors of the Pakistan People's Party government also joined the chorus for Zardari and Gilani to resign. "This is a great violation of our sovereignty, but it is for the president and prime minister to resign and no one else," Qureshi said at a press conference.

But the Government continued in a mode of denial and harped on the issue of violation of sovereignty. A resolution unanimously passed by joint sitting of the Parliament during which the opposition walked after over 10-hour marathon session on 8 May after the Osama killing said, "*After an in-depth discussion, including pr esentations made on the r elevant issues by the Dir ector General, Inter -Services Intelligence, Dir ector General (Military Operations) and Deputy Chief of Air Staff (Operations), the Joint Session of Parliament r esolved as under:*

Condemned the US unilateral action in Abbottabad, which constitutes a violation of Pakistan's sovereignty; Strongly asserted that unilateral actions, such as those conducted by the US forces in Abbottabad, as well as the continued drone attacks on the territory of Pakistan, are not only unacceptable but also constitute violation of the principles of the Charter of the United Nations, international law and humanitarian norms and such drone attacks must be stopped forthwith, failing which the Government will be constrained to consider taking necessary steps including withdrawal of transit facility allowed to NATO/ISAF forces; Expressed its deep distress on the campaign to malign Pakistan, launched by certain quarters in other countries without appreciating Pakistan's determined ef forts and immense sacrifices in combating terror and the fact that more than thirty thousand Pakistani innocent men, women and children and more than five thousand security and armed forces personnel had lost their lives, that is more than any other single country, in the fight against terror and the blowback emanating from actions of the NATO/ISAF forces in Afghanistan;

Called upon the Government to ensur e that the principles of an independent foreign policy must be gr ounded in strict adher ence to the principles of policy, as stated in Article 40 of the Constitution, the UN Charter, obser vance of international law and r espect for the fr ee will and aspirations of sover eign states and their peoples; Fur ther called upon the Government to r e-visit and r eview its terms of engagement with the United S tates, with a view to ensuring that Pakistan' s national interests ar e fully r espected and accommodated in pursuit of policies for countering ter rorism and achieving r econciliation and peace in Afghanistan; Affirmed the importance of international cooperation for eliminating international terr orism, which can only be carried forwar d on the basis of a true partnership appr oach, based on equality , mutual respect and mutual trust; Affirmed also full confidence in the defence forces of Pakistan in safeguar ding Pakistan's sover eignty, independence and territorial integrity and in over coming any challenge to security , with the full support of the people and Government of Pakistan. Reaffirmed the Resolution passed by the Joint Sitting of the Parliament on National Security held on 22 October 2008 and the detailed recommendations made by the Parliamentary Committee on National Security in April 2009." [8]

Denial was also written in the speech by Prime Minister Syed Yusuf Raza Gilani in the NationalAssembly on theAbbottabad incident, "Pakistan alone cannot be held to account for flawed policies and blunders of others. Pakistan is not the birth place of Al-Qaeda. We did not invite Osama bin Laden to Pakistan or even to Afghanistan. It is fair to ask who was Osama bin Laden and what did he personify?"

In an ominous warning he stated that this is not the end of the Al Qaeda or global terrorism as there was a lot of anger and frustration in the

---

[8] Terms of Engagement with US be reviewed. ht tp://www.dawn.com/2011/05/15/terms-of-engagement-with-us-be-reviewed-resolution.html

people which would have to be overcome. He said, "The myth and legacy of Osama bin Laden remains to be demolished. The anger and frustration of ordinary people over injustice, oppression and tyranny that he sought to harness to fuel the fire of terrorism in the world, needs to be addressed. Otherwise, this rage will find new ways of expression".[9]

This was the time the political opposition led by the PML N and its savvy leader Nawaz Sharif launched a broad side on the Pakistan Army. Using the budget session of the Parliament, a number of leaders of the Party called to question the efficiency of spending on the military. Outside the parliament in a number of public meetings Nawaz Sharif raised the same questions.[10] He attempted to cash in on the resentment against the Army in the masses as well as the general economic hardships imposed by an inflationary economy growing at just over 2 percent.

Not to be outdone the Army came out strongly against statements by PML N leadership in the National Assembly. In the 139[h] Corps Commanders Conference on 9 June 201 1, the Chief of the Army Staff Ashfaq Parvez Kayani who has been in the line of fire due to the somnolent state of the forces and failure for containing retaliatory attacks of the Al Qaeda was reportedly questioned by the Corps Commanders who are seen as the virtual, "parliament," of the country legislating strategic policy . Following the Conference, the Army also came out in a strongly worded statement released by the Inter Services Public Relations the same day.

The statement apart from a general review of the situation and action taken chastised, "some quarters," thus, "The participants noted with regret that despite briefing the Joint Session of the Parliament and deferring the ultimate findings to the Commission appointed by the Government, some quarters, because of their perceptual biases, were trying to deliberately run

---

[9] Anita Joshua. Elimination of Osama was indeed justice done: Pakistan.http://www.hindu.com/2011/05/10/stories/2011051055431200.htm

[10] Nawaz demands govt to present Agencies, Army budget in Parliament. http://www.pakistantoday.com.pk/2011/05/nawaz-demands-govt-to-present-agencies-army-budget-in-parliament/

down the Armed Forces and Army in particular. This is an effort to drive a wedge between the Army, different organs of the State and more seriously, the people of Pakistan whose support the Army has always considered vital for its operations against terrorists". [11] Very clearly these quarters were none other than Mr Nawaz Sharif and the PMLN.

The other aspect of emphasis during the Conference was Pakistan US relationship. Reflecting a general resentment over the 2 May incident and a general drawn down in the relations was indicated thus, "Army has drastically cut down the strength of US troops stationed in Pakistan. It needs to be clarified that Army had never accepted any training assistance from the US except for training on the newly inducted weapons and some training assistance for the Frontier Corps only". [12]

On intelligence cooperation with the United States it was indicated that this would be now on reciprocal basis, "The participants were also informed about the extent of intelligence cooperation with the US. It has been decided to share intelligence strictly on the basis of reciprocity and complete transparency. It has been clearly put across to US intelligence officials that no intelligence agency can be allowed to carry out independent operation on our soil". [13]

The US military aid to Pakistan was also attempted to be placed in perspective, "COAS also informed the forum that the often quoted figure of US $ 13-15 Billion utilised by the Army in last ten years is misplaced. Under the head of Coalition Support Fund (CSF), against a total sum of US $ 13 Billion expected from the US, only US $ 8.6 Billion have been received by

---

[11] 139th CORPS COMMANDERS' CONFERENCE ISPR Release No PR134/2011-ISPR Dated: Thursday, June 9, 2011. http://www .ispr.gov.pk/front/main.asp?o=t-week_view&id=1764#wv_link1764

[12] 139th CORPS COMMANDERS' CONFERENCE ISPR Release No PR134/2011-ISPR Dated: Thursday, June 9, 2011. http://www .ispr.gov.pk/front/main.asp?o=t-week_view&id=1764#wv_link1764

[13] 139th CORPS COMMANDERS' CONFERENCE ISPR Release No PR134/2011-ISPR Dated: Thursday, June 9, 2011. http://www .ispr.gov.pk/front/main.asp?o=t-week_view&id=1764#wv_link1764

the Government of Pakistan. The Government has further made available only US $ 1.4 Billion to the Army over last ten years. A relatively smaller amount has gone to Navy and PAF as well. The rest i.e. approximately US $ 6 Billion, have been utilised by the Government of Pakistan for budgetary support which ultimately means the people of Pakistan (The figures quoted here have been reconciled with the Ministry of Finance)". [14]

Finally the Statement called for a diversion of the US military aid for civilian purposes thus, "It is being recommended to the Government that the US funds meant for military assistance to   Army, be diverted towards economic aid to Pakistan which can be used for reducing the burden on the common man". [15]

The Pakistan Army thus concerned about a threat to it from the political class attempted to issue a stern warning to avoid confrontation. It also placed the Pakistan US relations in perspective highlighting a reduction in overall cooperation, military aid and intelligence sharing.

Richard A. Falkenrath's fears of a backlash from Pakistan over the killing of Osama Bin Laden in their territory came true with not just the government and the leadership ranting against violation of sovereignty but even the Army which is known to be closely knit behind the Chief, General Kayani seeing rumblings by the Corps commanders a powerful group of primary leaders who seem to determine the strategic course of the country This raised concerns of the Pakistan's nuclear arsenal in the days ahead, which is likely to be completely isolated from external surveillance and even expanded as leverage in the future. [17]

---

[14] 139th CORPS COMMANDERS' CONFERENCE ISPR Release No PR134/2011-ISPR Dated: Thursday, June 9, 2011. http://www   .ispr.gov.pk/front/main.asp?o=t-week_view&id=1764#wv_link1764

[15] 139th CORPS COMMANDERS' CONFERENCE ISPR Release No PR134/2011-ISPR Dated: Thursday, June 9, 2011. http://www   .ispr.gov.pk/front/main.asp?o=t-week_view&id=1764#wv_link1764

[16] Richard A. Falkenrath. Was Bin Laden the Easy Part? http://www.foreignaffairs.com/articles/67831/richard-a-falkenrath/was-bin-laden-the-easy-part

[17] Richard A. Falkenrath. Was Bin Laden the Easy Part? http://www.foreignaffairs.com/articles/67831/richard-a-falkenrath/was-bin-laden-the-easy-part

On the plus side Pakistan's double game has now been exposed to its own people as Stephen Cohen said, "The sky is dark with the chickens coming home to roost in Pakistan." Nothing is more galling to elite but exposure to its own constituency will this bring about a change in the Pakistani army and the intelligence establishment remains to be seen.[18]

How much the issues raised by the PML N will result in a positive turnaround for the country remains to be seen, for the ruling Pakistan People' Party (PPP) is standing behind the Army and the combination may be dificult to beat even in a general elections which is due in 2013. While the political dimension is a cause of concern, the terrorism one is also raising enough questions.

The Taliban Reacts in Pakistan

Just a few days before the killing of Osama and its backlash on April 23, 2011, Pakistan's Army Chief, General Ashfaq Kayani in his address to cadets at the Military Academy indicated, that "the terrorists' backbone has been broken."[19] The reaction of the Tehreek e Taliban Pakistan to the killing of Osama increased the level of terrorist attacks in the country placing General Kayani's statement to a severe test of credibility.

The first to face the brunt were 69 recruits of the Frontier Constabulary who lost their lives on 13 May The Taliban deliberately attacked the Frontier Constabulary which is the main paramilitary police force deployed in terrorist-infested area of Khyber Pakhtunkhwa and on the border with Afghanistan. The attack is significant as the rebels targeted new recruits most of them drawn from the Pashtun tribal belt. The message was therefore as much to the government as to the poor youth who had hopes of a future in the security forces.

On 16 May the Taliban claimed the killing of a Saudi diplomat in Karachi assassinated in an attack on his car. On 22 May came the complex attack

---

[18] http://www.guardian.co.uk/world/2011/jun/01/pakistan-osama-bin-laden-military

[19] Pak army has br oken terr orists' backbone: K ayani. ht tp://www.rediff.com/news/slide-show/slide-show-1-pak-army-has-broken-terrorists-backbone-says-kayani/20110423.htm

on the Karachi Naval air base PNS Mehran which saw the loss of two P 3 C Orion maritime reconnaissance aircraft apart from a number of naval personnel and civilians. This was a grim reminder of how the Taliban has been able to extend influence to the south taking advantage of the Karachi unrest. The group seems to have got a good foothold in the Pakistani commercial capital and is now targeting the Navy in particular with the third attack within a month. The Pakistan Armed forces had carried out some very effective shielding of the assets after the large number of suicide attacks including the one on the Army HQs. However some facilities as the naval bases and training centers were not that well protected.

The raid on the Pakistan Navy Base PNS Mehran was no doubt well planned and that it was in the ofing was evident as theTaliban had already tested the lax security arrangements of the Pakistan Navy in   April much before the killing of Osama when in three incidents Naval personnel were directly targeted.

In subsequent reports by investigative reporter Salem Shahzad who was later found killed after disappearing for over two days, it was revealed that the attack was possibly because the Navy had refused to release some personnel who had been apprehended for links with the   Al Qaeda. The Taliban continues to strike in the country in a series of attacks spreading from the tribal areas to the hinterland; a long counter terrorism challenge thus awaits the Army.

Impact on US Pakistan Relations

The most obvious consequence of Osama killing was on US Pakistan relations. The US had been concerned about the impact of the operation on relationship with Pakistan. For this reason senior officials were circumspect on whether the Pakistani government was aware that bin Laden was at this compound in Abbottabad. They emphasized that, "The relationship with Pakistan is an important one. It's also a complicated relationship and it's important that we find ways in the future to work togetherespecially on the counterterrorism front— This is a common fight. Bin Laden is responsible for supporting operations that have killed scores of Pakistanis as well, so there's a mutual interest in us working together". [20] Officials also did not commit initially on whether any links were found to other groups such as Lashkar-e-Taiba or Jaish-e-Mohammed the intelligence of ficial did not commit any thing nor did he confirm or deny that the information obtained was shared with countries as India. [21]

The Pakistani reaction was of betrayal by the Americans and the CIA and virtual suspension of contacts. [22] General Khalid Shameem Wynne, chairman of the Joint Chiefs of Staff, cancelled a scheduled visit to the United States. The ISI declared the name of the Station Chief of the CIA in Islamabad causing much rancor. These measures were followed by other signs of growing non cooperation.

Sensing Pakistani grievances, the US made sustained efforts to ensure that the relations did not completely break down. Secretary of State Hillary Clinton accompanied by Chairman Joint Chiefs of Staff Mike Mullens and Senator John Kerry were in Islamabad, so was US special envoy Marc Grossman for the second time during May. During her visit, Secretary of State Hillary Clinton at a press conference in Pakistan however did not mince her words when she said, "There is a momentum toward political reconciliation in Afghanistan but the insurgents continues to operate from safe havens here in Pakistan." The meetings were reportedly very frosty and Pakistani side in particular did not allow any exchanges with the media which has been the form on previous occasions. The presence of US Chairman JCS Admiral Mike Mullens would also indicate that on the military side there was much to talk about.

Ms Clinton made the point that the key challenge faced by Pakistan had to be overcome not just by cooperation on counter terrorism but also to

---

[20] Background Briefing with Senior Intelligence Official at the Pentagon on Intelligence Aspects of the U.S. Operation Involving Osama Bin Laden. U.S. Department of Defense Office of the Assistant Secretary of Defense (Public Affairs)

[21] Background Briefing with Senior Intelligence Official at the Pentagon on Intelligence Aspects of the U.S. Operation Involving Osama Bin Laden. U.S. Department of Defense Office of the Assistant Secretary of Defense (Public Affairs)

[22] Najam Sethi. Operation Get OBL. The Friday Times. Available at http://www.thefridaytimes.com/06052011/page1.shtml

build up capacity and will to fight. Senator John Kerry regarded as sympathetic towards Islamabad said, United States wants Pakistan to be a "real" ally. There were also reports of a meeting between Michael Morell, deputy director of the CIA with Inter-Services Intelligence chief Lt Gen Ahmed Shuja Pasha but these have not been confirmed possibly due to sensitivity of relations. Pakistan was reportedly playing a double game, reports indicate that in private they were congratulating the United States for the success and showing their willingness to cooperate while in public they adopted a virulent anti US stand.

The US clearly indicated that Pakistan should target militant leaders in the country or it would be constrained to again violate the sovereignty if need be. The choice before the leadership both civilian and military in Pakistan is therefore difficult either they hand over or taget the Taliban and Al Qaeda leaders themselves and face the ire of right wing parties many of whom offered public condolences to slain Osama Bin Laden or they have to await a similar response from the US on discovery of say Mullah Omar or Zawahiri either of whom and definitely the former is likely to be in Pakistan.

Pakistan however got strong support from two quarters, traditional friend China and the European Union (EU). EU foreign affairs chief Catherine Ashton supported Pakistan. "More than ever we need to underpin the democratic elected government of Prime MinisterYousuf Raza Gilani," said EU spokesman Michael Mann. The Chinese did not go as far as to condemn the US raid but supported Pakistan calling for respect of its sovereignty. Foreign ministry spokeswoman Jiang   Yu said national sovereignty "should be respected" at all times.The foreign ministry in Beijing explained that it "will continue to support Pakistan formulating…counter-terrorism strategies based on its own national conditions…."[23] "Pakistan is at the forefront of the international counter-terrorism effort. The international community should understand and support Pakistan," Jiang told a press conference. "We support Pakistan's position and understand and support Pakistan formulating and implementing a counter-terrorism strategy based

---

[23] Dan Blumenthal. China Breeds Chaos. http://online.wsj.com/article/ SB10001424052702304520804576344971111459988.html?KEYWORDS=dan+blumenthal

on its national conditions."[24]

Impact on Afghanistan

The Afghans also reacted to the discovery of Osama Bin Laden in Pakistan strongly. Afghan President Hamid Karzai said on May 2, 201 1 that the fight was not in Afghan villages, "We said many many times, and continue to say every day, the fight against terrorism is not in Afghanistan's villages, the fight against terrorism is not in the houses of poor and oppressed Afghans, the fight is not in bombing women and children. The fight against terrorism is in its sanctuaries, in its training camps and its finance centers Today, this has been proven right," thus indirectly pointing fingers at Pakistan. Haroun Mir, director of Afghanistan Centre for Research and Policy Studies, said "Pakistan has become very, very vulnerable. Frustration with Pakistan is greater than ever before." [25]

In America and Europe the war in Afghanistan was losing sheen as more body bags are flown home and the Taliban continue to hold sway in many parts of the country The death of Bin Laden however had the potential of making the larger campaign irrelevant. [26] Concurrently thus there was a call for a pull out of US troops in Afghanistan. The strong lobby which is against a general war and wants the same restricted to a counter terrorism campaign asked the President to hasten the troop withdrawal.

While the commencement of pull out of US troops from Afghanistan was anticipated the death of Osama Bin Laden added a sense of satisfaction if not victory. In a seminal speech to the nation on 22 June 201 1, The President claimed that the drawdown was, "from a position of strength," highlighting the success of killing of Osama Bin Laden and a half of Al Qaeda's leadership. He seemed to rely on a quote from a soldier to convey

---

[24] China urges world to back Pakistan in terror fight. http://www.dawn.com/2011/05/05/china-urges-world-to-back-pakistan-in-terror-fight.html

[25] Afghans Lash Out At Neighbor, Woo The US. Available at http://www.morningstar.co.uk/uk/markets/newsfeeditem.aspx?id=138501958365431

[26] Richard A. Falkenrath. Was Bin Laden the Easy Part? http://www.foreignaffairs.com/articles/67831/richard-a-falkenrath/was-bin-laden-the-easy-part

perseverance and determination of the US administration in pursuing its objectives, "The message," he said, "is we don't forget. You will be held accountable, no matter how long it takes." [27] He also claimed that the al Qaeda had failed in its narrative of portraying, America as a nation at war with Islam." [28] President Obama indicated good progress in Afghanistan with increase in the numbers of security forces, stability and peace that had resulted in a degree of normalcy with schools running and women and girls enjoying new freedom.[29]

Obama redefined objectives inAfghanistan as, "to refocus on al Qaeda, to reverse the Taliban's momentum, and train Afghan security forces to defend their own country".[30] He thus proposed to, "Remove 10,000 of our troops from Afghanistan by the end of this year, and we will bring home a total of 33,000 troops by next summerfully recovering the suge I announced at West Point. After this initial reduction, our troops will continue coming home at a steady pace as Afghan security forces move into the lead. Our mission will change from combat to support. By 2014, this process of transition will be complete, and the Afghan people will be responsible for their own security". [31]

At the same time he did underline the need to address the, "terrorist safe havens in Pakistan" and sounded a warning, "so long as I am President,

---

[27] The White House. Office of the Press S ecretary. Remarks b y the President on the W ay Forward in Afghanistan. June 22, 2011. http://www.whitehouse.gov/the-press-office/2011/06/22/remarks-president-way-forward-afghanistan

[28] The White House. Office of the Press S ecretary. Remarks b y the President on the W ay Forward in Afghanistan. June 22, 2011. http://www.whitehouse.gov/the-press-office/2011/06/22/remarks-president-way-forward-afghanistan

[29] The White House. Office of the Press S ecretary. Remarks b y the President on the W ay Forward in Afghanistan. June 22, 2011. http://www.whitehouse.gov/the-press-office/2011/06/22/remarks-president-way-forward-afghanistan

[30] The White House. Office of the Press S ecretary. Remarks b y the President on the W ay Forward in Afghanistan. June 22, 2011. http://www.whitehouse.gov/the-press-office/2011/06/22/remarks-president-way-forward-afghanistan

[31] The White House. Office of the Press S ecretary. Remarks b y the President on the W ay Forward in Afghanistan. June 22, 2011. http://www.whitehouse.gov/the-press-office/2011/06/22/remarks-president-way-forward-afghanistan

the United States will never tolerate a safe haven for those who aim to kill us".[32]

What was also very significant was that America was likely to look more inwards. President Obama stated in his address, "America, it is time to focus on nation building here at home. " Under the circumstances how the battle against theAl Qaeda and the other regional groupings that operate in its wake such as theTaliban, Lashkar eTaiyyaba and Haqqani group will be fought remains to be seen. [33]

Here the situation in the area needs some reiteration. The core of the terrorism bubble around Al Qaeda and the Taliban is in Afghanistan and Pakistan. A proactive military approach is being attempted to put down a militancy which is using terrorism as a strategy relying on modern bombs, improvised explosive devices, and assassinations and targeting civilian and military officials, subversion of the security forces and expanding ideology through use of coercive means. International Security   Assistance Force (ISAF) under a United Nations mandate and mainly comprising of countries of the North Atlantic Treaty Organisation [NATO] is leading the counter militancy campaign with theAfghan security forces capacity being built up slowly and steadily which is expected to be completed by 2014. Security would be transferred to the Afghan security forces with ISAF pulling out.

NATO commanders believe that the death of Osama will not impact the overall plan of counter militancy and pulling out by the ISAF. Deputy Civilian Spokesperson for NATO Chris Chambers claimed that there would be no change in the transition process, "That process has been ongoing since then and before the death of Osama Bin Laden. That process continues today to transfer security responsibility to theAfghan government and that process has not changed, the timeline has not changed and it will continue

---

[32] The Whi te House. Office of the Press S ecretary. Remarks b y the President on the W ay Forward in Afghanistan. June 22, 2011. http://www.whitehouse.gov/the-press-office/2011/06/22/remarks-president-way-forward-afghanistan

[33] The Whi te House. Office of the Press S ecretary. Remarks b y the President on the W ay Forward in Afghanistan. June 22, 2011. http://www.whitehouse.gov/the-press-office/2011/06/22/remarks-president-way-forward-afghanistan

unabated with or without the death of Osama Bin Laden. So there is absolutely no impact on transition at all.'[34]

Support to security and stability by NATO will continue to Afghanistan and Pakistan even beyond 2014. While counter terrorism challenges are expected to wither away, building and retaining the capacity of both Afghan and Pakistan security forces and maintaining balance in the political and security relations is likely to require the deployment of outside forces which is presently envisaged to be American under a well charted Afghan US strategic cooperation agreement for basing.

On the whole though announcement of Afghan pull out though gradual has led to concerns as many including the US military top brass which has called the President's pull out as aggressive feel that the situation may not be as rosy as has been painted during the national address. The al Qaeda is an organization which survives on empty spaces and failed governments and resuscitates itself by sustaining the momentum through a network of like minded groups. Once the Coalition pulls out of Afghanistan even if a large number of operatives are eliminated the ability to regroup and reemerge which has been its forte in the past may see its revival. Thus the overall uncertainty is likely to prevail and management of the militancy as well as Pakistan's commitment to contain the terrorism within its spaces and the rebel forces that operate from there in Afghanistan would have to be bolstered.

Managing Counter Terrorism Cooperation with Pakistan

A review of the various issues hitherto fore would underline that the crux of containing the Al Qaeda and global terrorism is Pakistani cooperation and determination to overcome the same in their own territory. Noted American scholar on Pakistan C Christine Fair flags numerous concerns that the US should have on Pakistan despite Bin Laden's death such as, "nuclear proliferation, security of peace-time positioning of Pakistan's nuclear

---

[34] IS AF Mission at Full Speed F ollowing Death of Al Qaeda Leader . Available at ht tp://www.isaf.nato.int/article/isaf-releases/isaf-mission-at-full-speed-following-death-of-al-qaeda-leader.html

weapons, mobilization during a crisis with India, command and control arrangement, much less the steepness of the escalation latter of an actual crisis with India among other salient concerns".[35]

The Al Qaeda network is very strong in Pakistan. Its numerous affiliates continually expand their sway with periodic terrorist attacks. Pakistan has a conglomerate of terrorist groups who can be ideologically divided as the Deobandi groups which include the Pakistani Taliban which has morphed into the Tehreek e Taliban Pakistan (TTP) mostly Mehsuds led by Baitullah Mehsud since 2004 until he was killed in a US drone attack in 2009 and thereafter by Hakimullah Mehsud, JM and Lashkar-e-Jhangvi (LeJ) Sunni groups targeting Shia again are Deobandi that is the Sipah-e-Sahaba-e-Pakistan (SSP), Lashkar-e-Jhangvi (LeJ)) and Deobandis who target Barelvis and Ahmediyyas.[37] A new trend of those who oppose the opponents of blasphemy law are emerging one of whom a guard of the late Punjab Governor Salman Tahseer killed him in broad daylight while on duty

The LeT morphed into two arms, the benign Jamaat ud Dawa (JuD), a charitable organization for all purposes which also received official donation from the Punjab government in Pakistan led by Mr Shahbaz Sharif, brother of former Prime Minister Nawaz Sharif, mentioned in the previous paragraphs. The LeT retains its terror folio led by Maulana Rehman Lakhvi accused of master minding the Mumbai terrorist attack.[38]

JuD on the other hand is able to organize rallies against the US demonstrations, which it did after the killing of Osama Bin Laden and the release of Raymond Davis, a CIA contractor who killed two ISI operatives and to support fundamentalist and extremist laws as the blasphemy law.[39]

---

[35] C. Christine Fair. Lashkar-e-Taiba beyond Bin Laden: Enduring Challenges for the R egion and the International Community. Testimony prepared for the U.S. Senate, Foreign Relations Committee. Hearing on Al Qaeda, the Taliban, and Other Extremist Groups in Afghanistan and Pakistan. May 24, 2011

[36] Ibid.

[37] Ibid.

[38] Ibid.

[39] Ibid.

The role of the LeT in domestic counter terrorism and militancy in Pakistan supporting the state has been highlighted by Fair who also seemed to suggest that the death of Osama Bin Laden on the LeT was not likely to be substantial as, " LeT's tight ties withAl Qaeda is not robust".[40] She also highlights that the relationship between the LeT and the Pakistani establishment is so strong that even if Indo Pakistan dispute, which another American scholar of South Asia, Stephen Cohen described as likely to last a 100 years, is resolved, the intelligence agency will not abandon this group primarily targeting India.[41]

Pakistan had placed counter terrorism cooperation in the dyad of a military threat from India.Today there are limited apprehensions given the positive indications from New Delhi in the past year or so after relations had virtually broken down after the terrorist attack in Mumbai called as 26/11 having occurred on 26 November 2008. There are also other issues. C Christine Fair highlights Pakistani resentment of Indo US nuclear deal and India's presence in Afghanistan as two major concerns in the country, "The U.S.-Indian nuclear deal has exacerbated Pakistan's concerns about India and angers Pakistanis who feel that U.S. alignment with its existential nemesis while Pakistan is at war with militants is an extreme insult," says Fair. The Pakistanis also lack an appreciation as per Fair that their strategy of fostering terrorism will not wear down India only harass it and that this is only resulting in resentment even in Jammu and Kashmir where the Deobandi tradition has no place in the syncretic Sufi culture.[42]

Noted Pakistan specialist, Stephen P Cohen states that the Pakistanis have more anti American sentiment than radicalism and this would be one of the reasons for continued resentment againstWashington. Cohen states, " I don't have evidence of Pakistan army as radical in the extreme sense. However, it has become more anti-American. Some sections of the army are more anti-American than they are anti-India. The obsession with India,

---

[40] Ibid.

[41] Ibid.

[42] C. Christine Fair. Try to see i t my way. http://afpak.foreignpolicy.com/posts/2011/05/24/try_to_see_it_my_way

on the other hand, is weakening Pakistan rather than strengthening it. Pakistan has a huge list of reforms that it should have made. [43]

C Christine Fair believes that the United States has limited options but to continue with cooperation with Pakistan even if there is evidence that the Pakistani establishment knew or supported Bin Laden. "Even if there were evidence of such complicity the uncomfortable reality is that it would change little if anything regarding U.S. interests in Pakistan. The United States does not have any real options to "cut off" Pakistan, despite the obstreperous calls to do so from corners of Congress and the U.S. government. The United States needs Pakistan for ground lines of control through which the vast majority of supplies move from Pakistans port city of Karachi through the length and width of Pakistan, before finally reaching U.S. troops in Afghanistan," she says. However if such complicity is discovered it would considerably weaken the position of the Army and the ISI and also expose its double dealings thereby bringing even greater pressure on it which would not be a bad outcome as a whole Fair feels. [44]

Fair however asserts that Pakistan is not likely to give up the Afghan Taliban, the Haqqani Network, Hekmatyar, or Lashkar-e-Taiba which are regarded as strategic assets against India. [45] Given this perspective, with Pakistan continuing to support groups which operate actively inAfghanistan the security in that country would remain a question mark despite the extensive efforts by the international community to bring about stability and upgrade the capability of the Afghan security forces. The sanctuaries and safe passage that is available to these groups in Pakistan and which cannot be effectively targeted will ensure their survival and facilitate operations to recapture Kabul once the Coalition forces leave post 2014.

On the ideological plane for the United States the challenge as per

---

[43] Interview with Malik Sir aj Akbar. 'Pak army mor e anti-American than r adical'.http:// www.dawn.com/2011/05/30/ pak-army-more-anti-american-than-radical.html

[44] C. Christine Fair. After bin Laden, Stll No Choice for US. with Pakistan. http://www.nbr.org/ research/activity.aspx?id=142

[45] Ibid

Richard A. Falkenrath is also dichotomy in its policies between realism and idealism or vital interests and values. "How to explain a values-based policy toward one Arab country while pursuing an interests-based policy toward another, more important Arab country? When and how to use the military power of a fractious coalition to protect a band of rebels from a wrathful, erratic dictator? How to support internal democratic reform in countries with no democratic political tradition and where political Islam is the most legitimate, cohesive alternative to the corrupt ancient régimes?, he states[46] This analogy may also be aptly applied to Pakistan where anti US sentiment sees the aid and assistance being given to create conditions for employment of military rather than assisting the Pakistani people. Resolving this dichotomy would thereby be important to improve the Pakistani approach towards the US.

Conclusion

The United States and its allies including Pakistan will continue to face the challenge from theAl Qaeda and its cohorts, the PakistaniTaliban, Haqqani network and Somali al Shahab who operate from areas which have been exclusively controlled by these groups as per noted American author Max Boot.[47] Weaving Pakistan into a larger counter terrorism grid appears to be the answer apart from inducing the security forces to undertake long term counter insurgency operations in the country.

Counter terrorism cooperation would have to be based on a risk reward mechanism, as no such paradigm exists at present the US finds itself virtually at the mercy of what decision makers in Islamabad and Rawalpindi particularly the latter decide should be the contours of the relationship. Implementing a programme of trust but verify for spending aid and structural reforms would be necessary rather than the carte blanche that has been

---

[46] Richard A. Falkenrath. Was Bin Laden the Easy Part? http://www.foreignaffairs.com/articles/67831/richard-a-falkenrath/was-bin-laden-the-easy-part

[47] Max Boot. Al Qaeda's Prognosis. Can Terrorist Groups Live Without Their Leaders? http://www.foreignaffairs.com/articles/67832/max-boot/al-qaedas-prognosis

given so far. [48] Targeting sub-state networks as political factions, NGOs and other civil society groups would also be important to win over their support.[49] This is said to be the trend ahead as United States and Pakistan have to increase covert efforts against al Qaeda, improve their intelligence collection capabilities and build trust to work in tandem to contain this threat.

There is also a need for innovating and new mechanisms such as regional and bilateral cooperation with the Shanghai Cooperation Organisation States including China, Russia and CentralAsian Republics and India. Beijing could play a more defining role provided the US and to some extent India could overcome apprehensions of greater Chinese influence in Islamabad. All said and done despite the success of Osama' s killing, that it happened in Pakistan without the knowledge of the government or military in that country seems to have raised more questions than answers in the larger context of countering terrorism emanating from theAfghanistan Pakistan region.

---

[48] Alexander Gal lo and Sc ott Helfstein. Springtime f or Jihadis. How Wil l Terrorism Evolve After Bin Laden? http://www.foreignaffairs.com/articles/67839/alexander-gallo-and-scott-helfstein/springtime-for-jihadis

[49] Alexander Gallo and Scott Helfstein. Springtime for Jihadis. How Will Terrorism Evolve After Bin Laden? http://www.foreignaffairs.com/articles/67839/alexander-gallo-and-scott-helfstein/springtime-for-jihadis

Chapter 6

Why Al Qaeda and Bin Laden Failed in India?

This Chapter essentially traces how the Al Qaeda and Bin Laden's efforts to penetrate India were defeated by highlighting the extensive attempts made over the years and the successful strategy employed by India.

Introduction

The killing of Osama Bin Laden on 2 May in Abbottabad, Pakistan once again directed global attention to the presence of Al Qaeda in South Asia. While the terrorist Group was well entrenched inAfghanistan prior to 9/11 and shifted base to tribal areas of Pakistan thereafter its main activities were in other regions of theWorld such as Iraq and the Maghreb. However discovery of the World's most wanted man, Osama Bin Laden in Pakistan, which was not surprising to many has again led to speculation of possibility of Al Qaeda's presence in India.

In some ways India could be considered an ideal ground for the Al Qaeda with origins of Deobandi and Salafi wings of Islam in North India in the early 20th Century. Given that theAl Qaeda in its hey day in the 1990's had attempted to make inroads in Jammu and Kashmir and extensively supported the, 'franchises,' Lashkar e Taiyyaba and Jaish E Mohammad amongst others also indicates a strong interest of the Group in India. While one argument is that elimination of Osama may effectively reduce potency of the organization, today's Al Qaeda is much more than Bin Laden howsoever monstrous he may have been. The group is now a violent extremist movement rather than a terrorist organization, thus its ability to conduct mayhem is far greater than hitherto fore with possibility of using WMD, particularly biological, chemical and radiological weapons to cause heavy casualties. Moreover past study of terrorism reveals that decapacitating a leader, even as dangerous as Osama seldom leads to the end of a terrorist group. However India's success in containing the Al Qaeda can provide some lessons on how the end of the group can be brought about globally.[1]

Al Qaeda – The Movement In South Asia

The rise and fall of Bin Laden and the trajectory of the al Qaeda has been covered in the preceding chapters. The fiery leadership provided by Bin Laden, his effective strategic communication capability , strong financial backup led Al Qaeda assume omnipresence in the nether world of terror across the globe. The networked organisation provided Al Qaeda survivability with a large number of flourishing subsidiaries. With pull out of Soviet troops from Afghanistan in 1989, the raison eitre for the Mujahedeen seemed to be over, but monstrous proportion assumed by groups as the Al Qaeda led to their expanding territorial span an

d targets. The Group also has the ability to spread ideology by using modern media, internet, social networking tools and blogs. This has enabled the group to develop what India's former National Security Advisor (NSA) Mr M K Narayanan has called the Al Qaeda, "mindset".

South Asia has the largest number of Muslims in the World, a majority of who are benign followers of the great faith Yet in the wake of the Afghan Mujahedeen war, the deviants, Taliban, Harakat ul Mujahedeen, Lashkar E Taiyyaba Jaish e Mohammad had assumed monstrous proportions. The rivalry between India and Pakistan in the Sub Continent has ideological roots in the, "two nation theory" of modern nation states divided on religious

---

[1] This chapter is based on an article by the author , *Al Qaeda in I ndia: Past, Present and Future,* Published in Defence and Security Alert June 2011. New Delhi

lines. The manifestation of this enmity into a strategy of state sponsored terrorism by Pakistan in the Indian provinces of Punjab and Jammu and Kashmir is now well established and has been covered in the previous chapter. The Al Qaeda found these ideal grounds for establishing it roots in the region employing the many terrorist groups as the Lashkar e Taiyyaba which had the support of the Pakistani state to advantage. Osama provided an organisational linkage by forming the International Islamic Front (IIF) in the 1990's which weaved in some of these groups.

The Al Qaeda in India –Past and Current Attempts

For Osama Bin Laden's aim of establishment of a global Caliphate, India was a natural extension with its lar ge Muslim population. The Al Qaeda saw communal riots in Mumbai in 1993 and Gujarat in 2002 fault-lines that could be employed to advantage by drumming up propaganda of exploitation of minorities. Jammu and Kashmir was another point of inflection. India's growing proximity to the United States and defence linkages with Israel made the country a priority for expansion of the network.

Al Qaeda could attract a number of groups who were operating in Jammu and Kashmir in the 1990's including, the Harkat ul Mujahidin (HUM), and Harkat ul Jehadi Islam (HUJI), Jaish e Muhammad (JeM) and Lashkar e Toiba (LeT) along with its political wing Jamaat ud Dawa. The Al Qaeda developed linkages with criminal groups as Dawood Ibrahim, master mind of the Mumbai bomb blast of 1993. Some of the groups as the HUM, HUJI, LET and JEM were a part of the IIFAl Qaeda influenced Kashmiri militancy by providing these groups training in camps, moneyarms and ammunition.[3] Osama also inducted the famed 055 Brigade to fight in Kashmir in June 1999. This force had approximately 200 experienced terrorists with exposure in Afghanistan.[4] The move came even as Pakistan sufered a setback during Operation Vijay in Kargil. 055 Brigade was seen as a boost to the morale of

---

[2] Asymmetrical Challenges to India's National Security. New Delhi: USI of India/ Knowledge World. 2002.P 206.

[3] Ibid, p 207.

[4] Ibid, p 207.

the insurgents fighting a losing battle in Jammu and Kashmir . A notable exception in the Kashmir Valley was the largest group, Hizbul Mujahideen comprising of locals who spurned Osama's outreach in no uncertain terms.

The Al Qaeda was however interested in India from the very beginning. Osama referred to Kashmir and Assam in his fatwa of August 1996 quoted in *Al Quds Al Arabi* , a London-based newspaper thus, "It should not be hidden from you that the people of Islam had suffered from aggression, iniquity and injustice imposed on them by the Zionist-Crusaders alliance and their collaborators; to the extent that the Muslims blood became the cheapest and their wealth as loot in the hands of the enemies. Their blood was spilled in Palestine and Iraq. The horrifying pictures of the massacre of Qana, in Lebanon are still fresh in our memory . Massacres in Tajakestan, Burma, Cashmere, Assam, Philippine, Fatani, Ogadin, Somalia, Erithria, Chechnia and in Bosnia-Herzegovina took place, massacres that send shivers in the body and shake the conscience". [5]

There are also numerous references to India in Al Qaeda messages, interrogation reports and internet references and also involvement in the Parliament attack in December 2001[.6] Al Qaeda operatives as Abu Zubaidah reportedly No 3 in the Al Qaeda hierarchy in 2002 had taken computer training in Pune before joining the organisation.[7] Yemen based Al Qaeda operatives had carried out dummy runs for a terrorist attack in Mumbai. [8] Osama's speeches on CDs with English sub titles have been recovered from Patna, Bihar and Bhojpur.

The Al Qaeda's brand name also started having impact with mysterious persons and groups claiming to belong to the organisation associating themselves with terrorist attacks such as the serial train blasts in local trains

---

[5] Bin Laden's Fatwa. "Declaration of War against the Americans Occupying the Land of the Two Holy Places. " Available at ht tp://www.pbs.org/newshour/terrorism/international/ fatwa_1996.html

[6] Note 2.p 219

[7] Swami, Praveen. Al Qaeda in India. Frontline. Jan. 05, - 18, 2002.

[8] Daily News Analysis Report. 10 August 2007 Available at http://www.ipcs.org/ Aug_07_terrorismGeneral.pdf.

in Mumbai on 11 July 2006, which had caused 187 fatalities. An unknown person calling himself Abu al-Hadeed, claimed to be from the Al Qaeda and congratulated the group which had carried out blast. Another odd group led by one Abu Abdul Rehman claiming to be the chief of al-Qaeda Fil Hind or al-Qaeda in India surfaced on Friday 8 June 2007 with a tape to the Current News Service in Srinagar with the message, "W e declare righteous holy war against India on behalf of God the great in which Jammu and Kashmir will be the launch pad for holy war in India."[10]

The Al Qaeda also attempted two interventions as per media reports referring to Mr S D Pradhan former chairman of the joint intelligence committee. The first was a reconnaissance between February and April 2007 by a 10-member team of Bangalore, Mumbai and Goa which was later caught in Algeria. In 2008 Saudi Arabian students of the Islamic Students Congregation in Pune were given a sermon on Osama' s preaching by a Sudanese national who is suspected to be an Al Qaeda agent.[11]

Even as India weathered the complex Mumbai terror attack on 26 November 2008, there was extensive national debate over response towards Pakistan after terrorists were identified from that country. Al Qaeda's military commander in Afghanistan, Mustafa Abu Yazid released a tape warning against an offensive in February 2009. "India should know that it will have to pay a heavy price if it attacks Pakistan," Mustafa Abu Yazid said, "The Mujahideen will sunder your armies into the ground, like they did to the Russians in Afghanistan."[12]

The next warning came exactly a year later . The Indian counter terrorism establishment led by Home Minister Mr P Chidambaram had

---

[9] Gentleman, Amelia. Qaeda claim of Kashmir link worries India. International Herald Tribune. 13 July 2006.

[10] Bin Laden's Fatwa. "Declaration of War against the Americans Occupying the Land of the Two Holy Places. " Available at ht tp://www.pbs.org/newshour/terrorism/international/fatwa_1996.html

[11] India puts pressure on Pakistan, stays alert. Available at http://www.livemint.com/2011/05/02225956/India-puts-pressure-on-Pakista.html?atype=tp

[12] Bill Roggio. Al Qaeda threatens India with 'humiliation' if Pakistan is attacked. February 9, 2009. Available at http://www.longwarjournal.org/archives/2009/02/al_qaeda_threatens_i.php#ixzz1Llcp7s5p

succeeded in staving off a major terrorist attack in the country till February 2010, when in Pune a bomb attack in the German Bakery frequented by foreigners killed 17 persons. Immediately following the attack a message reportedly by Ilyas Kashmiri the Al Qaeda supposed commander for the region warned, in a message, "We warn the international community not to send their people to the 2010 HockeyWorld Cup, the Indian Premier League and Commonwealth Games – to be held in New Delhi later this year. Nor should their people visit India – if they do, they will be responsible for the consequences." The Indian establishment duly warned conducted these events successfully indicating to the group that the space for terrorist violence had been considerably constricted. The mention of Pune in the conference held on the so called Kashmir Solidarity Day on 4 February by terrorist groups in Pakistan Occupied Kashmir which reportedly includedAl Qaeda operatives as well raises the needle of suspicion of linkages of the organisation with the Pune blasts. [13]

Recent reports in Wiki leaks indicate that theAl Qaeda had planned to bomb an Indian airline in 2001-2002. The report quoted by Indian daily , Indian Express read, "Abdul Azia, an Algerian member of the Lashkar-e-Taiba and an al-Qaeda courier picked up by the US in 2002 who said that his mission was to 'kill Indians in India', has been recorded as saying that the ISI 'allowed' fighters to fight inside India. [14] Another media report indicated that Al Qaeda had attempted to procure altimeter watches as triggers for targeting an Indian airliner. [15]

The Peruvian Financial Intelligence Unit (FIU) has also recently highlighted that theAl Qaeda was routing money from Europe to the Peruvian capital of Lima and then to India and at least one case per month was being noticed in 2009 as per FIU head Enrique Saldivar disclosed! [16]

---

[13] Al Qaeda vows more attacks across India. February 16, 2010. Available at http://www.zeenews.com/news604454.html

[14] Gitmo files reveal al-Qaeda plan to bomb Indian airliner . http://www.indianexpress.com/news/gitmo-files-reveal-alqaeda-plan-to-bomb-indian-airliner/787408/0

[15] 'Al-Qaeda planned to bomb an I ndian airl iner'. 8 Ma y 2011. A vailable at ht tp://www.timesnow.tv/Al-Qaeda-planned-to-bomb-an-Indian-airliner/articleshow/4372635.cms

[16] Al-Qaeda routing money to India via Europe. Available at http://www.hindustantimes.com/StoryPage/Print/670044.aspx

A review of the incidents reported above would denote that while the Al Qaeda has failed to penetrate India despite the many fault lines this is not for want of trying. From Kashmir in the 1990's to Pune in 2010, footprints of the Group have been noticed by the Indian security establishment. In most of the casesAl Qaeda has acted through proxies as it lacked indigenous leadership. Recent reports indicate nomination of Ilyas Kashmiri as the first commander ofAl Qaeda in India. Kashmiri has a very dangerous reputation as a terrorist organizer and may be able to activate the dormant network to greater effect. Though some reports now indicate that Kashmiri may have been killed in a US Drone Strike in Pakistan's tribal areas this has not been confirmed. The creation of Lashkar supported group, the Indian Mujahideen is another dangerous trend in this direction. So we have to view the future ahead with caution.

The Future

As the proverbial saying by the Taliban goes, "you have the watch but we have the time." Terrorist groups have infinite patience and perseverance. The Al Qaeda targeted the United States from the early 1990's and could carry out a major attack only in 2001. Similarly India will have to maintain a vigil despite low penetration of the Group and the death of Bin Laden. The likely rise of Mohammed Ilyas Kashmiri, who unlike other seniorAl Qaeda commanders has experience of fighting in Jammu and Kashmir and thus can effectively organize major terrorist major acts, is also a warning. Kashmiri is reportedly associated with the Harakat-ul-Jihad Islami's (HuJI) and led the so called Brigade 313 operations in Jammu and KashmirThe importance given to Kashmiri is evident from an audio message by al-Qaeda's former senior commander Mustafa Abu al-Yazid posthumously indicating that Kashmiri is the leader of, "Qaedat al-Jihad in Kashmir ."[17] Analysts also feel that Kashmiri fills up the major void for the organization of an indigenous

---

[17] Seth Nye. Al-Qaeda Exploits K ashmir Conflict to Expand Oper ations to I ndia. Terrorism Monitor Volume: 8 Issue: 39. October 28, 2010. A vailable at http://www.jamestown.org/ programs/gta/single/?tx_ttnews[tt_news]=37093&tx_ttnews[backPid]=457&no_cache=1 http://www.jamestown.org/programs/gta/single/?tx_ttnews[tt_news]= 37093&tx_ttnews[backPid]=457&no_cache=1

leader and may shift focus to a terrorist attack in the hinterland with Jammu and Kashmir militancy on the ebb.[8] However if the recent reports of Kashmiri having been killed in a US drone attack prove to be true, than to an extent this threat would be that much reduced.

The David Headley episode is also indicative of the larger designs of groups as the LeT. Headley had carried out reconnaissance of a variety of locations including oil installations, the country's premier defence institution, National Defence College and the Prime Minister's residence. The Group may use its own resources or take assistance of the LeT or the Indian Mujahideen for a terror attack in the country in the future as the threat will remain in being for some time to come. On the other hand there is some support to the Group amongst mainly marginalized separatist leaders as Syed Ali Shah Geelani who led funeral prayers for Bin Laden in Jammu and Kashmir.[19] Taking advantage of the liberal Indian milieu, Mr Geelani has been actively following a deviant path, the radical agenda of such leaders will have to be effectively countered. However this time he may have overplayed his card of radicalization as Osama has very little sympathy in Jammu and Kashmir.

Why Al Qaeda Failed orWill Fail in India?

Despite the forebodings highlighted above, theAl Qaeda may succeed only in an episodic attack in India and there are no reasons to fear the movement taking roots in the country. Bin Laden's isolationist mindset as he was the only sibling of the wealthy Saudi family who did not travel abroad for study was particularly weak in identifying with other cultures. Thus despite many

---

[18] Seth Ny e. Al-Qaeda Exploits K ashmir Conflict to Expand Oper ations to I ndia. Terrorism Monitor Volume: 8 Issue: 39. October 28, 2010. A vailable at http://www.jamestown.org/programs/gta/single/?tx_ttnews[tt_news]=37093&tx_ttnews[backPid]=457&no_cache=1

[19] Hundreds join JuD prayers for 'martyr' Osama. Available at http://www.indianexpress.com/news/hundreds-join-jud-prayers-for-martyr-osama/785406/0 but Policing Remains Unchanged. Paper was presented in the International Conference on Radicalisation Crossing Borders, Global T errorism R esearch Centre (GTR eC), P olitical and Social Inquiry (PSI), Monash University, 26-27 November 2008.

attempts Kashmir's largest and indigenous militant or ganisation, Hizb ul Mujaheedin never joined the Al Qaeda network. This strain is evident across the country as Indian Muslims including prominent clerics of the Deobandi School have spoken strongly against terror, violence and suicide attacks.

The clerics at Deoband and Jamiat Ulema e Hind publicly rejected violence and terrorism in a series of fatwas first in the   All India Anti-Terrorism Conference, held on 26 February 2008 which was converted into a national fatwa by a declaration in the capital Delhi on 31 May 2008. This stated, "Islam is a religion of peace and harmony. In Islam, creating social discord or disorder, breach of peace, rioting, bloodshed, pillage or plunder and killing of innocent persons anywhere in the world are all considered most inhuman crimes." The defining phrase however was when the fatwa declared, "Islam was born to wipe out all kinds of terrorism and to spread the message of global peace." [20] These statements reflected the general sentiment of Indian Muslims brought up in a culture of pluralism.

This is not to say that there are no religious tensions in the country or groups as the Indian Mujahideen or the Students Islamic Movement of India popularly known as SIMI do not find space in the Indian anti state discourse. But this strain of extremist violence is based more on socio-economic grievances rather than religious discord which   Al Qaeda preaches. Thus Osama Bin Laden's philosophy is unlikely to find much favour in India in the near future.

Bin Laden perhaps never understood the Indian socio cultural ethos and values practicising syncretism as opposed to monotheist absolutism preached by the Al Qaeda. This is evident as the security establishment has been able to successfully neutralise the militancy in Jammu and Kashmir with support of the people of the S   tate. The, "Foco," and "Detonator ," theories spawned by Bin Laden by imposing an Islamist veneer has no traction in India.

---

[20] Kamala Kanta Dash. The F atwa against Terrorism: Indian Deobandis R enounce Violence but Policing Remains Unchanged. Paper was presented in the International Conference on Radicalisation Crossing Borders, Global T errorism Research Centre (GTReC), Political and Social Inquiry (PSI), Monash University , 26-27 November 2008.

Conclusion

While Bin Laden is dead, it will be some time before the Al Qaeda will be truly defeated. Of the many ways in which terrorism ends, the death of a leader is possibly one of the weakest vectors for change.   Thus the Al Qaeda will continue to haunt security planners and counter terror forces across the World including India. Al Qaeda's singular failure in making an impact in the largest democracy with the second largest Muslim population in the World remains a mystery to many. The group never appreciated the pluralist and secular ethos which has rejected the likes of Bin Laden over the centuries. The Al Qaeda could only depend on its network with groups as the LeT. Will Bin Laden's death and a shake up leadership with Ilyas Kashmiri likely to assume a major role in the Majlis change this approach remains to be seen. However till Pakistan's approach to terrorism is ambivalent and terrorist infrastructure remains in being across the border, the Al Qaeda will remain a threat in being though its ideology will not find any takers in India.

Most importantly however for the purpose of this study the salient lessons that India provides in defeating the Al Qaeda are how to meet the ideological challenge by deftly dissecting the warped narrative and use universal Islamic thought rooted in larger human values of pluralism, non violence, empathy and compassion towards fellow beings through indigenous schools of preaching which have credibility amongst the Muslim community

Chapter 7

The Future of al Qaeda and Terrorism

In this chapter using scenario planning technique four possible
futures on the trajector y of terr or have been pr ojected namely, "Atlas
Shrugged," "Poisoned Chalice," "House of Cards," and "Bottled Genie".

"To deal with the future we have to deal with possibilities Analysis will
only tell us 'What is'."

Edward de Bono, Parallel Thinking

Introduction

The assassination of Osama Bin Laden in Abbottabad on 2 May 2011 was
a seminal event in the history of counter terrorism, just as 9/11 had been a
decade ago. Intricacies of the operation as well as significance of Bin Laden'
extermination have been examined in detail in previous chapters. What is
important is to visualize the future of terrorism in general and the al Qaeda
in particular, for the latter has come to signify a paradigm of rebellion which
is spawning individual and group clones across the world. There have been
many statements on the trajectory of global terrorism and the al Qaeda
after Bin Laden's death. The most recent one was by newly anointed United
States Defence Secretary Leon Panetta who had the distinction of taking
out Bin Laden as the chief of the Central Intelligence Agency (CIA). On

---

[1] Scenario Planning. Guidance Note. Foresight Horizon Scanning Centre, Government Office
for Science. Government Office of Science UK. London. 2009.

his first visit to Afghanistan as the Defence Secretary in July 2011, Panetta expressed the confidence that the defeat of Al Qaeda was within reach. The reason proffered was decimation of its leadership with less than two dozen key leaders now left in Pakistan,Yemen, Somalia, and NorthAfrica. "If we can be successful at going after them, I think we can really undermine their ability to do any kind of planning to be able to conduct any kinds of attack on this country (United States)," Panetta told reporters on his way to Kabul.[2] Mr. Panetta's assertions would be no doubt based on facts to which he would have privileged access.

Yet the ground situation does not denote that al Qaeda and much less terrorism is in general retreat. The death toll from terrorist attacks continues to cause alarm despite a receding trend and new areas are impacted each year with other forms such as piracy and maritime terror adding to the overall threat spectrum. This is not surprising and reflects the overall pattern since 9/11 when theAl Qaeda and theTaliban were chased out ofAfghanistan but were able to rejuvenate and have sustained their campaign of mayhem across the world particularly in South and West Asia. These organizations are increasingly threatening America and the West with newer challenges, be it that of cartridge and innerwear bombs or explosives implanted in the body to avoid detection.[3] The number of terrorist groups across the World continues to remain high and the prospects of terror as a security threat receding at best remains uncertain. The reason for the same is not far to seek, the raison d'etre of al Qaeda' s extremist violence, ideology has not been defeated. This was evident when Bin Laden's death was not mourned even officially in many countries inWest Asia or NorthAfrica while functions mourning the same were held in many parts of theWorld including in parts of liberal pluralist democracies as India.[4]

---

[2] Panetta says U.S. is 'within reach' of defeating Al Qaeda. Available at http://www.latimes.com/news/nationworld/world/la-fgw-panetta-kabul-20110710,0,5988043.story?track=rss

[3] Terrorists May Be Turning to Human Bombs, U.S. Warns. Available at ht tp://www.foxnews.com/politics/2011/07/06/us-warns-terrorists-might-try-to-plant-bombs-inside-people/

[4] Special prayer held in Kolkata for al-Qaeda chief Bin Laden. Available at http://www.allvoices.com/contributed-news/9001943-special-prayer-held-in-kolkata-for-alqaeda-chief-bin-laden down loaded on 11 July 2011.

Thus envisaging the outlook of terrorism with certitude in the years ahead will remain a key challenge for the security community   . It may therefore be worthwhile to make use of future techniques to foresee the threat of terror a decade or so ahead and envisage different states in which the World may find itself in say 2020 living with or without al Qaeda. The scenario planning technique is used for this purpose as explained in subsequent paragraphs.

Scenarios as Crystal Ball Gazing

Scenario planning is a future technique used for strategic forecasting. Simply speaking scenarios are stories of the future describing how the World may appear for the purpose of advance planning. This provides medium to long term perspective to evolve strategic options. [5] Scenarios have been used extensively by research organizations as Rand Corporation in the United States as well as Stanford Research Institute. In the private sector Shell Corporation has also used scenario building for projecting oil prices. Thus the technique can be adapted to situations of uncertainty where possible pathways cannot be clearly visualized and variables are numerous and unpredictable.

Scenarios provide a high degree of flexibility in visualizing outcomes and also facilitate adopting right strategies as well as indicate how trends denote the future. Thus positive indicators would denote an optimistic and negative, deteriorating reality of the situation ahead. Scenarios also facilitate strategies to contain and neutralize the threat which in this case is of terror across the globe. The technique involves detailed examination of principal factors which affect the given problem known as drivers or factors which are independent variables. Uncertainty in progression of factors denoted by trends determines the alternate futures. While theoretically there can be unlimited scenarios however to enable realistic planning are generally brought down to a reasonable number say four to five.

---

[5] Scenario Planning. Guidance Note. Foresight Horizon Scanning Centre, Government Office for Science. Government Office of Science UK. London. 2009.

[6] Ibid

Given the nature of terrorism as a socio political problem scenario building is considered appropriate for developing alternate futures with particular reference to the Al Qaeda. The main factors considered relevant to build scenarios projecting the future of terrorism based on the study hitherto fore are, Ideology and Narrative, Population Support, Leadership, Organisation, Support structures and State Support to Terrorism. Detailed evaluation of these drivers, uncertainties and trends is being carried out as per succeeding paragraphs. [7]

Ideology, Narrative and Population Support

Terrorism is differentiated from crime by its political character and ideological moorings. The Al Qaeda ideology of use of indiscriminate violence across the globe to establish an Islamic Caliphate is appealing only to a miniscule minority, its core followership. This is however adequate for the group to attract deviants to its fold who carry out suicide attacks killing innocents without any qualms. Terrorism thus does not require mass support however it requires sympathy of the population and towards that end the narrative is as important as the ideology. The al Qaeda story as has been brought out in previous chapters as well is to exploit the sense of persecution in the Muslim community, expand anti West sentiment, and create hype over hot button issues as Palestine and target secularism and pluralism. The aim is to capture imagination of the people by carrying out vicious terrorist attacks against objects of general hatred or disaffection. Constant hammering of the narrative by using modern media to create a wave of publicity by vile acts of terror enables the group to gain support of that critical mass that enables it to survive and thrive. Conspiracy theories are also used to effect to expand the plot giving it numerous dimensions thereby exponentially expanding the impact particularly in societies with low education levels which are dependent on traditional means of communication such as religious leaders. Internet chat rooms are also used to effect to spread conspiracies thereby expanding

---

[7] Scenario planning is best carried out by a group. The framework provided in this chapter is developed based on a study by the author of te   rrorism over the past few years and includes participation in many discussions on the subject of terrorism and counter terrorism, though not specifically related to the scenarios covered.

the size of the population influenced.

Al Qaeda also employs traditional conflicts in a region such as between India and Pakistan to advantage by using the narrative of contest of ideologies as the two nation theory or states divided based on religion to its own advantage.[8] Pakistan has fallen into this ideological trap while India has rejected the same spurning al Qaeda as has been seen in the previous chapter

The ideology and narrative thus remain one of the key drivers for sustaining terrorism. Some of the trends that would determine the trajectory of ideology and the narrative are existing political idioms and narratives surrounding these, ideologues who espouse them and their intonations, information and media for proliferation in the target population.

Taking these one by one, the growth of extremist preaching of an ideology, be it religious or say ethnic separatism will denote possible rise in support to use of violence as an instrument. Concomitantly deradicalisation of a society would be a contra trend which can counter the extremist narrative and would indicate lack of support to the ideology and the narrative. Ideologues who preach violence such as al Qaeda' s Jordanian cleric Abu Muhammad al-Maqdisi and how far and wide their voice reaches will also dictate support. While most ideologues will have a local impact the use of violence by their political protagonists as Bin Laden will result in global prominence. On the contrary moderate voices will gain traction as influence of the ideology is softened and overall tone of extremism is lowered in a society.

Information and media is an essential tool that terrorist groups employ to effect and which the al Qaeda is very adept at. More over it finds the target audience through dedicated media such as the glossy magazine, "*Inspire*," which is launched to specifically attract American youth. The wide span of media today given proliferation of newspapers, web sites, television and radio stations provides incidental traction. The use of innovative means such as FM radio in Swat province of Pakistan denotes how these

---

[8] Robin W. Winks, Alaine M. Low. The Oxford history of the Br itish Empire: Historiography. OUP. New York. 1999. P 257.

are exploited by the deviants to advantage. Maulana Fazlullah leader of Tehreek-e-Nafaz-e-Shariat-e-Mohammadi (TNSM) was named as, "Mullah Radio," for introducing broadcasts with extremist preachings in 2006. Thus the increase or decrease of these sub facets would also denote the rise or fall of ideology of extremism.

While terrorism does not necessarily require population support where the same is used as tactics in militancy the latter would need support of the people. This is achieved either willingly or through coercion and propaganda. The battle for the hearts and minds in this case becomes important for the security forces in addition to a large foot print to facilitate operations.

Leadership

Any movement which fosters violence requires strong and inspirational leadership. To attract a group of youth to carry out a suicide attack requires a high degree of trust in the leader even though the young men may be uneducated or semi literate. Leadership will be primarily required in three dimensions, ideological as has been highlighted hither fore, political and the military. The political connects the ideological and the military as represented by Bin Laden and is thus the most important of the three. Ideological leaders may be few whereas political and military leaders have a hierarchy which is well established. The leadership of all major terrorist groups follows a command chain. The leadership structure, numbers, hierarchy and command chain are various components that would have to be measured to denote the strength of an organization. In the case of the al Qaeda it is the Majlis which has leaders looking after various functions such as training, finance, indoctrination, propaganda and so on. Succession in such organizations is therefore smooth. Except for Bin Laden, the al Qaeda has been nominating successors to replace other commanders who have been killed such as Zarqawi in Iraq within 24 hours.

---

[9] Richard A. Oppel Jr. Pir Zubair Shah, Ismail Khan Radio spreads Taliban's terror in Pakistani region. Available at http://www.nytimes.com/2009/01/25/world/asia/25iht-25swat.19645197.html accessed through Wikipedia.

Leaders who are a part of the Majlis will not expose themselves and will also be sheltered by other members even at the cost of their lives, thus reaching these is extremely difficult. The individual personality of leaders will indicate their authority. No doubt Bin Laden's influence was extensive despite his absence from the mainstream for almost a decade which was due to the force of his cultivated personality. Decapacitation of a leader(s) and/or neutralizing his influence is an essential facet of countering this factor Decapacitation can be through physical elimination whereas neutralization could be in various forms including winning over by the government to marginalizing by lack of popular support. However how much this will contribute in neutralizing large organizations as theAl Qaeda is not clear so far.

Organisation

A terrorist organization has a number of components - cells, branches or affiliates. These can be large but lesser in number or small but spread across a vast geographic space. These would be mostly covert except for large sanctuaries such as tribal areas of Pakistan where some of the groups as the Tehreek e Taliban operated openly until commencement of US drone attacks. The typical Al Qaeda set-up as has been highlighted comprises of branches spread across continents, similarly theTaliban has a network that is spread acrossAfghanistan and tribal areas of PakistanA large organization will be extremely difficult to neutralize and the al Qaeda and theTaliban fall in this category. These may require a combination of counter militancy and counter terrorism efforts to neutralize. The number of fighters and over ground supporters are another component of this facetAgain the larger the numbers the greater will be the influence of the group.

However the potential may not be restricted purely to numbers for the al Qaeda is considered far more potent than other terrorist groups despite lesser numbers. This is also evident from the number of successful attacks it has been able to carry out and large number of casualties that have been inflicted by it across the globe. Infrastructure such as training and media are other sub factors.   The Al Qaeda is reportedly having an elaborate facility in the tribal areas of Pakistan where fighters from all over theWorld

127

come down for training and indoctrination. This network can be shared as between al Qaeda and the Taliban to achieve economies of scale as well as outsourced to other groups. Neutralising these sanctuaries and hideouts will remain an important component of counter terrorism. Smaller terrorist organizations operate in cells which are either sleeper, semi active or active and will also have a support base of over ground workers. Intelligence and information will be the key to neutralize their influence.

Support Structure

The support structures for terrorism are financial, arms and media networks. The financial arrangement can be substantive and can comprise of legitimate business whose proceeds are used for terrorism. Drug networks have emerged as the single largest financial base of terrorist groups with Afghanistan being the hub not just for South Asia but Central Asia and even Russia feeling the heat. Money laundering, criminal activities such as extortion and kidnapping, piracy and so on also support terrorist groups. These activities could be categorized as criminal terrorism and are being extensively used by terrorist groups in India's North East today to sustain support. Increasingly terrorist groups are creating front organizations for collecting money.

For instance the Lashkar eTaiyyaba has a front organization the Jamaat ud Dawa which collects funds through coin boxes placed at important locations around a city, donations and even government funds by running charitable schools and hospitals. During the floods in Pakistan in 2010, the Jamaat ud Dawa was in the fore front for relief but operated under the name of Falah-e-Insaniyat taking advantage of the devastation in the countryside and lack of state capacity to deliver[10] Targeting terrorism would imply neutralizing all activities that enable such organizations to sustain be it financial, criminal or logistics such as provision of arms and ammunition.

---

[10] Pakistan flood aid from Islamic extremists. http://www.telegraph.co.uk/news/worldnews/asia/pakistan/7957988/Pakistan-flood-aid-from-Islamic-extremists.html

State Support to Terrorism

State support covert, overt or incidental has emerged as an important factor for survival and growth of terrorism. Rogue states as Afghanistan was in the times of Taliban overtly supporting the Al Qaeda who had a free run of the country and could thus expand their network which finally led to 9/11. However most states that are a part of the international system, support terrorist groups covertly through their intelligence agency This practice is not restricted to a single country but is prevalent across the board. Thus the Indian intelligence agency Research is alleged to have supported the LTE.[11] CIA and Saudi intelligence bankrolled the Afghan Mujahideen through Pakistani ISI.[12] The ISI in turn gained extensive experience and fostered the Taliban which was used to gain strategic space in Afghanistan until the Americans rolled back the same in October 2001 launching Operation Enduring Freedom. Similarly the ISI fostered militancy in Jammu and Kashmir from the 1990's leading to a virtual state of war or No War No Peace between India and Pakistan for almost two decades.

States could also become tacit or incidental supporters of terrorism by providing ungoverned space to terrorist groups to operate. The tribal areas of Pakistan and Afghanistan, Somalia and Yemen are some of the regions where lack of governance is providing scope to terrorist groups to operate with impunity. Regaining control of this space is necessary for which physical presence of security forces and government authority is essential. This can happen with what is classically known as, "boots on the ground," or physical presence of a certain quantum of security forces which has been calculated by various norms such as persons per thousands of population for effective control. Restoration of authority of civil government in these areas through normal governance means is also important.

---

[11] Siddharth Vardarajan. The Road Ahead for India and Pakistan. The Hindu. 5 October 2009. New Delhi p 9.

[12] Harvey W. Kushner. Encyclopedia of terrorism. Sage. 2003. P 21.

Uncertainties

The main challenge in mapping the future is uncertaintyGiven the nature of factors which drives terrorism how these will project, ascend or descend will be indicated by trends which in turn will denote scenarios. For example ideological support for terrorism is difficult to predict. Some indications could be increase in proclivity to accept violence by extremist elements in marginalized communities across the World. On the contrary encouraging moderation will move youth away from extremism.A structured approach can be undertaken as being done recently by the Pakistan Army which is experimenting with deradicalisation centers in the SwaValley. An international seminar on deradicalisation was addressed by the Prime Minister Yousaf Raza Gillani and the Chief of the Army Staff General Pervaz Kayani in Swat in July 2011; however despite these measures containing spread of extremism in the days ahead remains uncertain. [13]

Similarly while there is a general anger against the US andWest in the Islamic world after the killing of Osama Bin Laden, whether this is a temporary phenomenon or something more tangible remains to be seen.A reduction in the Al Qaeda's capability for propaganda seems to be the immediate trend post Osama killing but whether this will be sustained is also unclear. The capability of leadership to uphold the Al Qaeda with a new command element under Zawahiri in power is also not well establishedAs has been brought out earlier, the new US Defence Secretary Leon Panetta claimed that strategic capability of the Al Qaeda will be soon neutralized. How far this will be achieved when the organization is spread from South Asia to the Middle East is questionable. Mr. Panetta's statement could be seen more as a proclamation of confidence and hope rather than certitude. Similarly observations could be made about the organization and support structures which are presently strong despite sustained action being taken to target these over a period.

State support to terrorism also remains a key uncertaintyFor instance

---

[13] People, state institutions to jointly eliminate terrorism; Gilani. 7 July 2011. Available at http://www.primeministerofpakistan.co index. php?page= detail &p=news&id=855

Pakistan despite the ignominy of Abbottabad has not demonstrated a shift away from the dangerous path of fostering groups directed against Afghanistan and India. Instability in countries as Yemen where the al Qaeda has a strong presence is a major concern, for stabilization in the near term remains a chimera which may not be achievable. Similarly Somalia despite intervention of an African Union led force supported by the United States through a barrage of drone based missile attacks will remain a security black hole in the near future. These regions will thus provide state support or environment for terrorism though some changes internal and external give hopes of betterment of the situation. Thus these uncertainties may dictate varying scenarios in the future.

Building Scenarios

To reiterate factors which will impact terrorism are, Ideology and Narrative, Population Support, Leadership, Organisation, Support structures and State Support to Terrorism. These can be categorized in three broad groupings based on inter relationship as follows: –

(a) Group 1 - Ideology and Population support.

(b) Group 2 - Leadership and Organisation.

(c) Group 3 - Support structures and state sponsorship.

The influence of these factors can be envisaged as global, regional or national/local and in terms of degree categorized roughly as high, medium and low. A threat posed beyond a single continent as that by   Al Qaeda today in more than one group outlined above would be categorized as global. Where the spread of influence of an organization is in more than one country or transnational the threat is categorized as regional and when confined to a country as national or local. Thus the Taliban or the Lashkar e Taiyyaba could be categorized as regional while the Tehreek e Taliban with activities within Pakistan as national or local threat A quantifiable metrics for degree of intensity of influence as high, medium or low would have to be developed separately. One that is commonly used is that of number of violent incidents, fatalities, injuries and type of attacks. This is an exercise by itself and can be evolved by the principal stake holders addressing the challenge. However some trends to denote the same have been indicated in this chapter subsequently.

The possible scenarios emerging from a discussion of the above could be represented by a matrix as per Table below based on global, regional or national/local spread and high, medium or low intensity. While the matrix may denote a large number of possibilities, a realistic assessment could narrow down these to a handful which are being discussed in the succeeding paragraphs.

Factor	High Threat			Medium Threat			Low Threat		
	Glob-al	Regional	Natio-nal/L-ocal	Glo-bal	Regional	Natio-nal/L-ocal	Glob-al	Regional	Natio-nal/L-ocal
Ideolo-gy and Narrati-ve									
Popula-tion Suppo-rt.									
Leader-ship									
Organi-sation									
Support structu-re									
State Support to Terrori-sm									

Scenario 1 - Atlas Shrugged

Where ideology and narrative of an or ganization is spread globally, with other factors also having an expanse that is inter continental even if the degree of threat is high, medium or low this will be categorized as a global challenge as it would have to be met by a combination of states rather than singly. In such a case the high threat scenario was possibly experienced by the World immediately after 9/11 followed by the London, Madrid and Bali bombings when Al Qaeda's shadow loomed lar ge. The group's affiliates were also active in various parts of the   World including the   Taliban in Afghanistan, the Lashkar eTaiyyaba in Jammu and Kashmir in India and so on. Such a globally expansive threat called as the, "Atlas Shrugged," scenario could emerge in the years ahead if all vectors attain a high degree of intensity due to collapse of determination of the current international order to meet the challenge with unity.

In such cases even if the threat regionally such as say in Europe or in South East is categorized as either median or low and not necessarily high, the specter of spread will always remain a concern. Such a scenario could also be classified as globally expansive, regionally/nationally restrained or regressive. The activities of theAl Qaeda today could fall within this paradigm spread in three main areas of influence as   Af Pak tribal belt,   Arabian Peninsula and Maghreb with the possibility of engulfing the Horn ofAfrica in the near future. Concomitantly regional or national threats are being posed in other parts of the world such as by the   Tehrek e Taliban in Pakistan or Left Wing Extremists in India. This end state of the, "Atlas Shrugged [14]," scenario could be relative anarchy due to collapse of reason and controls of governance, isolation and withdrawal of the global order in the face of threat of terrorism partially or even totally.

The Atlas Shrugged scenario could be represented by a possible matrix as given below.

---

[14] The name is derived from Ayn Rand the Objectivist philosopher's famous novel. Atlas Shrugged. Random House. 1957 .

Factor	High Threat			Medium Threat			Low Threat		
	Global	Regional	National/Local	Global	Regional	National/Local	Global	Regional	National/Local
Ideology and Narrative	y					y		y	
Population Support.	y					y		y	
Leadership	y					y		y	
Organisation	y					y		y	
Support structure				y		y		y	
State Support to Terrorism				y		y		y	

To summarise a high threat of spread of ideology, population support and leadership as well as oganization globally, a medium challenge in some pockets and low threat in other regions could be representative of the Atlas Shrugged scenario. Total collapse of the global order to terrorism could be an unrealistic scenario but intercontinental manifestation cannot be ruled out, hence the depiction is considered probable. Post 9/11 such a scenario did emerge and the possibility of the same coming up in the years ahead cannot be ruled out in case the will to combat terror weakens.

Scenario 2 - Poisoned Chalice

A scenario that could be opposite of the above is globally restrained or regressive but regionally expansive and is named as, "Poisoned Chalice". This is possibly obtained in the Af Pak region where the spread of the

Taliban as a genre to include the Mullah Omar led or Quetta ShuraTaliban, the Haqqani group and Hizb e Islami which operate inAfghanistan and the Tehreek e Taliban carrying out activities in Pakistan have a transnational influence in various dimensions be it organizational, leadership or incidental state support due to availability of vast ungoverned space in the tribal areas. While the Al Qaeda influence here is limited but its support structures for training and indoctrination are effective to some degree while it has reach in other parts of the globe such as the Arabian Peninsula and the Maghreb. There is potential of spread globally but at a given point of time is restrained. The end state of the, "Poisoned Chalice," scenario could arise from a death wish which engulfs states and governments in a region thereby leading these to anarchy and collapse even though other parts of theWorld will be stable or may encounter mild pangs of instability . The Poisoned Chalice scenario could be represented by a matrix as indicated below-

Factor	High Threat			Medium Threat			Low Threat		
	Glob-al	Regional	Natio-nal/Lo-cal	Glob-al	Regional	Natio-nal/L-ocal	Glob-al	Regional	Natio-nal/L-ocal
Ideology and Narrati-ve		y				y	y		
Populat-ion Support.		y				y	y		
Leader-ship		y					y		
Organis-ation		y					y		
Support structure		y				y	y		
State Support to Terroris-m					y	y	y		

135

To summarise in the Poisoned Chalice scenario a specific region could expect high threat while correspondingly globally the same may be low or even non existent. On the other hand nationally or locally in some parts outside the region the threat may be even high or medium though the latter has been depicted in the matrix above.

Scenario 3 - House of Cards

In a third contingency terrorism may be globally and regionally regressive, but nationally or locally expansive. Such a scenario is named as, "House of Cards." In a future context where the Al Qaeda possibly withers away and the situation in Afghanistan is stabilized with intervention of the International Security Assistance Force (ISAF) and build up of Afghan security and governance capability but that in Pakistan deteriorates, such a scenario could well emerge. Thus, though the threat is limited globally and regionally it is potent nationally or locally with possibility of re-emergence through contagion. This cannot be ignored by states on the periphery. Similarly in case the threat from religious extremism is contained across the globe and region, but that of Left Wing Extremism spreads in India again a similar situation may emerge. The end state of the, "House of Cards," scenario represents fragility of situation in a state and if it collapses the domino effect could lead to a fall in other areas as well. The House of Cards Scenario could be represented by a matrix as given opposite.

Factor	High Threat			Medium Threat			Low Threat		
	Global	Regional	National/Local	Global	Regional	National/Local	Global	Regional	National/Local
Ideology and Narrative			y				y	y	
Population Support.			y				y	y	
Leadership			y				y	y	
Organisation			y				y	y	
Support structure					y	y	y		
State Support to Terrorism					y	y	y		

To summarise in the House of Cards scenario depicted above the main challenge is restricted nationally or locally while regionally and globally the threat may be low or even non existent. Yet some of the factors such as support structures and state sponsoring to terrorism may be at a medium level thereby having the potential of collapse in case the state under high threat succumbs to pressure.

Scenario 4 -"Bottled Genie"

While underlining downslide in vectors leading to various scenarios depicted above, possibility of a setting of stability due to successful counter terrorism efforts globally cannot be ruled out. This is depicted as the, "Bottled Genie," scenario wherein threat of terrorism is largely contained, but given intrinsic human proclivities for dissent, rebellion and violence, the devil is bottled so to say and if allowed to escape will return with vengeance. Thus the end state of the, "Bottled Genie," scenario would represent containment of forces of terrorism across the global. This is the best case scenario that the World should strive for with a bottom up approach with each state and region working to free itself of the threat of terror.

Trend Mapping

The most common basis for evaluation of threat of terrorism is the state of physical activity such as incidents of violence, fatalities and so on. Similarly counter terrorism success is measured in terms of kills achieved. This is a rough and ready method and may not indicate the reality to the fullest degree. Thus a relatively more effective measurement of trends of various drivers is necessary to evaluate the manner in which either of the scenarios stated above develop. These trends could be, positive or negative and would have to be mapped separately. Some of the possible trends are discussed as per succeeding paragraphs.

Ideology and Narrative -Trends

Growth of radical thought is a function of development of alternate philosophies, ideologues and structures fostering these such as seminaries for spreading religious extremism and media. Given human proclivity for diversity of thought, alternate philosophies are inevitable, how much these are bound by rationality of reason rather than the gun will determine support to extremist violence. Absence of a viable political ideology may also breed extremism hence a healthy debate of ideas in society is necessary. A vacuum in these will be a good indicator of a possible tipping point for unreason to prevail. Presently there are enough grounds to fear the rise of radically right wing as well as left wing ideas.

Determining the extremist strain of an ideology is some times difficult and poses a challenge. For instance organizations as the Hizb ut Tahrir[15] or

---

[15] Hizb ut Tahrir. About Us. A vailable at http://english.hizbuttahrir .org/index.php/about-us

138

Tablighi Jamaat[16] though fundamentalist in their ideology claim that they disavow violence while the latter even propounds that it does not indulge in political work. Similarly the Salafi ideology followed in Jammu and Kashmir bans violence and extremism, so in some ways determining the ideological inclinations of an organisation may become difficult. Yet these organizations have been accused of extremism and the Hizb ut Tahrir remains banned in many countries.

Leaders are an important medium of radicalization. Thus targeting ideological leadership by questioning credibility and rationality will be logical. Which side the balance tilts will determine the trend towards or away from radicalization. Ideological mediums will also include nodes such as religious seminaries or madrassa which have become a significant tool for the spread of radical Islamic thought such as the Salafis, Deobandis and the Ahl e Hadees sect. A growth in number of madrassas and students attending these as well as the curriculum followed will be a good indicator as to which way the wind is blowing. For instance in Bangladesh the government led by Awami League set into motion a programme of deradicalisation of the madrassas in 2009.[17] These were supported by the government with regulated syllabus and introduction of modern education tools including computers. Financial support to some of the madrassas from extremist organizations from foreign countries was also stopped thus making these dependent on the government and amenable to regulatory controls.

Syllabus and lessons in text books of schools and colleges are also a powerful tool for framing ideas in the young and thus will indicate the trend towards or away from radicalization.

Existence of a special deradicalisation programme formal or informal and the political support that it has will also be an important determinant.

---

[16] While there are many authoritative works on the Tableeghi Jamaat a summary of profile of the organization is pr ovided by Khalid Hasan. T ableeghi Jamaat: al l that y ou know and don't. Available a http://www.dailytimes.com.pk/default.asp?page=2006\08\13\story_13-8-2006_pg3_4

[17] Indian newspaper Pioneer praises Bangladesh's anti-militancy campaign. Available at http:/ /www.priyo.com/story/2011/jan/07/17122-indian-newspaper-pioneer-praises-bangladeshs-anti-militancy-campaign

Political ideologies of the regime in power will be a major trend indicator Where the regime supports fundamentalists even tacitly these organisations will be able to survive and thrive. On the other hand the more pluralist and secular is the party in power the lesser will be the threat of support to extremism in the country Again taking the trend from Bangladesh it is evident that the Awami League seen as secular brought about significant shift in the overall approach of the government in the country to crack down holistically on ideology of extremism and its support structures thereby containing its growth.

The final element is media which as a tool is possibly universally available today and would be difficult to deny to terrorist groups as much it is to dissident in a society This factor is evident from the ability of rebels to beat restrictions imposed by authorities even in authoritarian societies where violation of norms could lead to death. However continued targeting of the media used by denial of services, hacker attacks and limitation of sophisticated media in the hinterland when used effectively can lead to restricting availability of these means to propagate deviant ideology.

Population Support -Trends

As indicated earlier support of a miniscule minority of the population is enough to foster terrorism but the overall sentiment in society has to sustain the narrative. Pakistan remains a salient example of this phenomenon. Right wing religious parties have been consistently defeated in elections in the country whenever they have lacked support of the army , yet the overall mood of the population is two fold, religious fundamentalist and anti US. Thus Ahmediyyas are persecuted in the country and any opposition to the blasphemy law invites bitter opposition including assassination most significantly that of Mr Salman Tahseer governor of Punjab province by his own body guard.[18] Such an atmosphere is conducive for extremist elements

---

[18] Blasphemy laws in Pakistan proscribe defamation of all recognized religions but are said to be applied only to the official religion Islam. Sentiment against those who seek review of the blasphemy law is very strong in the country These are essentially enshrined in provisions of the Constitution and Penal Code.

as the Al Qaeda and the Tehreek e Taliban to survive as they can live in a sea with non resistant water indicating lack of opposition if not support. Thus trends may be denoted in different ways, lack of opposition, passive support and active support. Where terrorism is an instrument of militancy support of the population would be much wider and here winning hearts and minds is important. Such a campaign generally follows the path of development rather than ideological reframing and thus may or may not work in the long term. On the other hand where it is based on a transforming idea that supports rebellion, it is more likely to succeed.

Leadership - Trends

Leaders are an important factor in terrorism; they frequently have a larger than life image as signified by Bin Laden. Zawahiri also occupies a similar though to a lesser degree place in the minds of the group'followers as well as the general public. Thus terrorism's association with leadership is an important link. How strong this link is will be difficult to quantify? The key leaders are normally underground and in today's media rich environment seldom have to appear in public. Muppala Krishna Rao or Ganapathy the General Secretary of the CPI M or Naxals as they are known in India has not been seen in public, nor does he circulate video clippings like Osama Bin Laden but has been directing the struggle against the state ef   fectively. Neutralising leader's links with the group as well as the masses will deny them the ability to influence their activity

Actions taken physical or otherwise for curbing or targeting leaders may project a positive trend.   Yet an organization which has a functional hierarchy may not be impacted by decapacitation of the leaderThe al Qaeda demonstrated this trend till end June though the period may be considered to short as Osama Bin Laden was killed only on 2 May In the same vein, the Maoists in India have suffered leadership hemorrhage in the past two years as the government has expanded the campaign in Central India, however this does not seem to have affected the organization in a major way though the activities have seen a setback.

141

Organisation - Trends

Large terrorist groups as the al Qaeda have a well established organization. This is spread over many countries. The geographic expanse, number of cadres, training base, weapons available, organizational unity and so on are some of the trends which will determine organizational strength. The training infrastructure of an organization for instance may be extensive to include facilities, literature and indoctrination material all of which could be based on the web. It may thus take many years to defeat a militant or terrorist organization given ability of the guerillas to survive in the wilderness as well the sea of humanity in urban areas. Information of the organization and targeting each facet apart from eliminating the flow of new recruits would denote a positive trend. The smaller an organization the easier or quicker it would be to neutralize, on the other hand large organizations can be split into smaller groups thereby enabling their destruction.

But terrorist organizations are dynamic in nature and will continually fractionalize or merge. The Al Qaeda operates on the theory of an expanding base by enlarging its presence outward from a possible toehold, the proverbial camel in a tent strategy . The merger of the People' s War and the Maoist Communist Centre in India in 2004 is seen as a defining trend in rise of Left Wing militancy. Similarly terrorist groups also have the capacity to resuscitate the salient example being that of the   Al Qaeda which recovered with a vengeance in 2006-07 from the post October 2001 rout.

Support Structures - Trends

Terrorism support structures are varied to include financial networks, drug smuggling rings, criminal hubs, arms and people trafficking groups and so on. The size, scope and capacity of these to generate say funds for the terrorist groups would determine how long they will be able to sustain these.

State Support to Terrorism

State support to terrorism is an important indicatorCovert or overt support is difficult to define and no government is likely to openly acknowledge that it shores up a group or ideology unless it is defined under the paradigm of support to groups fighting for freedom. Thus Pakistan has been overtly providing moral and material support to terrorism in Jammu and Kashmir on the plea of siding with aspirations of the local population for accession to Islamabad. The mode and form of this support could be in terms of political, sanctuaries, training, arms, financing and so on and each would have to be targeted separately. On the other hand existence of an environment of anarchy which facilitates existence of terrorist groups can be determined through indices such as Failed States Index or Global Peace Index.[19] Inability of the state to deliver basic services in a modern society including guarantee of life, limb and property and a functional judiciary independent of state authority will denote poor governance. The US Department of Defence or Pentagon has also developed a framework for assessing safe havens which includes, geographical, political, civil and resource considerations to determine the vulnerability of an area for this purpose.[20] Using such measures possibility of safe havens can be roughly predicted.

Wild Card and Catastrophic Events

Scenario building is challenged by wild card and catastrophic events such as the Arab Spring or the assassination of Bin Laden. Despite the wide bank of research in futuristic assessments, there are no viable models where such events can be factored in and the influence will be mainly determined by the experience of those undertaking the exercise. One way is to base scenarios exclusively on long term trends, as this exercise claims to be, wild card events may have a limited impact. At the same time it is prudent to revisit the exercise on occurrence of such events.

---

[19] Failed States Index is anannual ranking prepared by the Fund for Peace and published by Foreign Policy of the world's most vulnerable countries. Global Peace Index (GPI) is produced by the Institute for Economics and Peace and gauges ongoing domestic and international conflict, safety and security in society, and militarization.

[20] Robert D Lamb. Ungoverned Areas and Threats from Safe Havens. Final Report of the Ungoverned Areas Project Prepared for the Office of the Under Secretary of Defense for Policy. Office of the Deputy Assistant Secretary of Defense for Policy Planning. Available at http://www.cissm.umd.edu/papers/files/ugash_report_final.pdf

Conclusion

Four possible scenarios on terrorism which can portray a comprehensive threat interweaving the global, regional or national/local dimension have been suggested herein named as Atlas Shrugged, Poisoned Chalice, House of Cards and Bottled Genie. Terrorism just like other socio political projections will remain highly uncertain thus mapping trajectory is no doubt hazardous yet within the paradigm of these four scenarios it is felt that the overall rubric can be accommodated. Resolve of the global and regional community and individual nation states to combat terrorism is important if the Atlas Shrugged scenario is to be avoided and a Bottled Genie one to be achieved. However modern liberal democracies be it global powers as the United States or regional majors as India tend to demonstrate episodic drive to meet the challenges from terrorism whereas a sustained campaign virtually on the lines of a, "war," without naming it to be so is necessary if the scourge of terror is to be overcome. Continuing with the theme strategies to counter terror will be discussed in the subsequent chapter.

Chapter 8

Strategies - Bottled Genie Scenario

"In the final analysis, it is the unity and strength of the people that will defeat these efforts to divide our people and destroy our civilized way of life".

India's Prime Minister Dr Manmohan Singh,
After serials blasts in Mumbai on 13 July 2011

This chapter discusses strategies that would lead to the ideal scenario to contain the genie of terrorism covering political, operational, internal security and counter state support dimensions. A case study of South Asia is included to highlight the challenges faced in counter terrorism cooperation at the global and regional level.

Introduction

Assassination of Al Qaeda leader Osama Bin Laden was a singular achievement and was possible due to determined national leadership, perseverance of United States intelligence and unique assets possessed by the American Special Forces which were efectively employed for the strike. The operation violated sovereignty of Pakistan which was tenable only by the United States. These unique attributes denote that it would not be possible for any other country to carry out a similar operation. More over despite the assertion by many particularly from the US defence and intelligence community, the Al Qaeda is unlikely to wither away with the elimination of Bin Laden. This is the received wisdom of those who have studied terrorism and practiced counter terrorism as has been brought out in the previous chapters as well. Thus a comprehensive approach is necessary to achieve the desirable, "Bottled Genie Scenario," to contain terrorism in the coming decade.

In Chapter 2 a number of studies on how terrorism ends have been outlined. To reiterate the various means to neutralize terror and its roots are leader decapacitation, negotiations, suturing support base, change in political goals, military defeat by a combination of policing, intelligence and armed action and failure of the movement contrasted by success. For ending state support to terrorism, cooperation, diplomacy economic and trade sanctions, development aid and assistance and use of military force or war have been considered. Given that failure is not a viable option for the global community strategies proposed for countering terrorism to lead to the Bottled Genie or control and containment scenario can be categorized fourfold as follows:-

(a) Political.

(b) Operational.

(c) Internal Security or Homeland Security.

(d) Countering State Support.

The challenge in countering terrorism is as much cultural as technical for solutions invariably probe the socio political domain. These strategies will be regulated by basic principles which are unity of effort, cooperation, comprehensive approach and long haul. These precepts are universally applicable at the global, regional and national as well as local levels. Unity of effort includes planning and action by state as well as non state actors, the latter in fact play an important role given the socio-political dimension of the challenge. While state may exercise the hard options, non state actors as religious organizations, spiritual leaders and community elders can provide the voice of reason which will defeat the narrative of extremism and strive for moderation.

A relative concept is cooperation which is a concern given bureaucratic inefficiency in modern governance and inherent resistance to change. Cooperation between nations can be attained through regional security structures while between agencies particularly intelligence through information sharing mechanisms and compatibility of stake holders. Building security partnerships is also identified as one of the core principles in the United States National Counter Terrorism Strategy released in July 2011.[1] To achieve cooperation, mechanisms such as Unified Commands would have to be created headed by local political authority . India has had considerable success through this model in Jammu and Kashmir as well as in Assam.

A comprehensive approach and time are two principles essential to neutralize groups as the al Qaeda. While these are have been accepted are seldom followed particularly at the global and international level. For instance North Atlantic Treaty Organisation (NATO) has adopted a comprehensive strategy in Afghanistan however despite deployment of vast quantum of material and intellectual resources progress remains uncertain due to excessive and exclusive focus on the military. Similarly while a long time span is of essence in containing militancy, the date for a final pull out has already been announced as 2014. This will militate against a logical conclusion, as the guerrillas have to wait and watch (sic) for the antagonists to withdraw to declare victory and set upon the local government. These factors cannot be understated. Against this backdrop various counter terrorism strategies are discussed in succeeding paragraphs.

Political Strategies

Political Will and Population Support

First and foremost, terrorism like war is regulated by politics which has many dimensions. Countering terrorism particularly when carried out in alien territory would necessitate building internal political will to sustain a campaign despite setbacks. To the people at home, the stream of body bags may

---

[1] US Government. National Str ategy for Counter T errorism. June 2011.

diffuse the overall goal, especially when improved homeland security will reduce the threat of terror. Yet allowed to grow unrestrained, terror in far away land could come to haunt a country . Afghanistan provides a contemporary backdrop as support for deployment of troops in the 40 plus coalition under International SecurityAssistance Force (ISAF) has reduced at home; there is an outcry for pull out. This may create conditions which are favourable for return of the Taliban and in turn the Al Qaeda. The overall political strategy has to include sensitizing public opinion to possible long term threats and necessity for deployment of troops abroad.

Similarly building mass opinion even at the national level is important. While this may appear easy given that a government is seen to always act in its own interest, various socio political interests in society may prevent coagulation of public opinion to counter terrorism. This is the foremost task of the political elites. Liberal democracies are prone to act reactively while authoritarian states may do so proactively but in that case high handedness may lead to mass resentment which will again feed terrorism. So a balanced approach would be required.

Negotiation and Reconciliation

Negotiation and reconciliation is a well recognized strategy to contain and neutralize terrorism. Willingness of both parties to negotiate is necessary. The guerrillas may be willing to parley either when they are in an advantageous position or when they have been exhausted. Conciliation and compromise can also be undertaken during the interim period of a conflict to reduce the number of combatants in rebel forces. This is the current approach in Afghanistan along with that of politicizing the Taliban. Thus when to negotiate remains a critical political cum military decision which will be determined by each side considering the advantages that may accrue from talks. Negotiation and reconciliation could follow various paradigms as suspension of operations, cease-fire and talks followed by a political solution, the UN disarmament, demobilization and reintegration (DDR) model, or Disbandment of Illegal Armed Groups (DIAG) used in Afghanistan or any other suitable construct which facilitates cessation of hostilities, peace and stability. It may comprise of two components, reconciliation with the higher leadership and reintegration of the fighters.

Such programmes require holistic support of the government and local communities, a permanent organization for implementation, budgeting and a well structured plan for relocation of rebels in civilian jobs. When support is lacking, the program is likely to fail. Citing an example from Afghanistan Matt Waldman, fellow at the Carr Center for Human Rights Policy at Harvard University outlines the failure of the DDR programme as it had, "minimal lasting impact, was subverted by militia commanders or local strongmen, and many participants were not genuine ex   combatants...Indeed, many second tier commanders who were reintegrated under DDR were deeply dissatisfied with the process and considering remobilisation. They not only lost income, but also their former authoritystatus, and public respect derived from the resistance". [2]

On the other hand Nepal is an example of successful negotiation and reconciliation strategy which was worked internally to get the Maoist guerrillas to the talks table in 2006. The initial success led to formation of a Maoist led government elected by the people in 2008; however fragility of the political process has delayed full implementation.This also denotes the importance of early closure from opening of peace talks to disarmament and rehabilitation of fighters as well as accommodation of the leaders in the political mainstream. Extended talks are unlikely to be fruitful as is evident in the long peace talks between the Naga rebel outfit National Socialist Council of Nagaland (Isac Muivah) and the Indian government which started in 1997 but have failed to conclude due to political dfferences [till June 2011]. This has resulted in guerrillas continuing to hold arms and indulging in acts of criminal terrorism. Thus early closure of negotiation and reconciliation process is important.

It is generally believed that groups which have local or limited aims are more amenable to political reconciliation than those with more expansive

---

[2] Matt Waldman. Golden Surrender: The Risks, Challenges, and Implications of Reintegration in Afghanistan. http://aan-afghanistan.com   index.asp?id=731.

objectives. Al Qaeda's ideology of establishing global caliphate may not make it open to negotiations. However affiliate groups such as the Taliban are being actively engaged by the United States amongst other countries in Afghanistan and have shown some inclination to parley though there are no definite trends till June 201 1 that any group from the loosely connected coalition will come over ground. Splitting a large group by employing ruse and inducements may be one of the sub strategies that may bring those amongst the conglomerate who want to compromise to the negotiating table. However for a lasting solution ideological reconciliation is necessary

A structured organization will be essential to implement a large reconciliation programme. For implementation of the Afghan Peace and Reintegration Plan (APRP) in Afghanistan for instance an elaborate organization under the President has been drawn up indicated as an elucidation, as per Figure 1.[3] (*See opposie page*) Given the strength of the Taliban at 25,000 to 30,000 a lage organization may be necessary for smaller groups a committee or task force could also be created to manage reconciliation. In India for instance a Cease Fire Monitoring Group has been nominated for progressing talks with Naga rebels, while in some cases the existing administrative machinery inAssam for instance is handling talks with the United Liberation Front of Assam with relevant accretions.

---

[3] http://aan-afghanistan.com/index.asp?id=751

President

P&R High Council (HC)
Deputy to the HC/Head of Joint Secretariat, NSA, Ministers of Mod.,
MoI, MoFA, MoF, MAIL, MoTA, IDLG, Head of Ulema Shura,
Speakers/Deputies of Meshrano/Ulasi Jirgas, elders and influential
figures-including women

JCMB - Security Standing Committee
Key GoA and IC stakeholders, including ISAF

Executive Director and Joint Secretariat

Trust Fund Management Committee
MoI, Head of IS, one rep. from donor community. Technical support will be provided by UNDP. TF will have two windows

Technical Assistance

Monitoring and evaluation Section

Legal Section

Technical Assistance

Deputy of Reintegration

Deputy of Administration / Strategic communication

Joint Secretariat

Deputy of Reconciliation

Security Committee

Development Committee

Peace, Reconciliation and Reintegration Provincial Committee
Under the leadership of PGs, will be consisted of Head of Provincial
Ulema Shura, ANA, ANP, NDS, MRRD, MAIL, MoTA, ISAF/PRT,
UNAMA Regional Rep and other influential figures

Peace and Reintegration District Committee
ANA, ANP, NDS, Head of district council, district Ulema Shura,
Reintegration Program authorities and ISAF

Technical Assistance for the Secretariat and Program Implementation

Figure 1

151

Counter Ideology, Narrative, Propaganda, Media

General

Political strategy will have to counter terrorist ideology and narrative, beat the propaganda and disrupt media tools employed for spreading the message of violence. Contemporary terrorism is primarily based on three ideologies, ethnic separatism, right wing or religious extremism and left wing violence. Political strategies will have to deal separately with nuances of each by developing an alternate discourse be it of nationalism, the most commonly used, identity integration which primarily deals with separatism and moderation to combat religious extremism. Existing ideologies, idioms and circumstances will have to be employed to advantage to defeat the terrorist agenda. For instance theArab Spring provides an ideal opportunity to negate Al Qaeda's ideology of change through violence and as is being covered in detail in subsequent parts of the chapter Similarly development through an electorally elected government and legislative democracy will beat Left Wing ideology. Countering radicalization by emphasizing on predominantly moderate strains in every religion remains a viable option to counter right wing extremism. Some other essential facets are covered as per succeeding paragraphs.

Countering ideology is about details and use of correct language. There is much debate on the use of word, "war" to describe the campaign against terror. The United States National Counter Terrorism Strategy released in July 2011 highlights the issue thus, "The United States deliberately uses the word "war" to describe our relentless campaign against al-Qa'ida. However this Administration has made it clear that we are not at war with the tactic of terrorism or the religion of Islam.   We are at war with a specific organization—al-Qa'ida".[4] While there is no doubt that counter terrorism will have to be undertaken on a war footing directed against terrorist groups and not against a religion, theAl Qaeda misrepresents the use of the word, "war," as persecution of Islam by the West. The delicate nuancing in the

---

[4] US Government. National Str ategy for Counter T errorism. June 2011.

counter terrorism strategy document is unlikely to be understood by the man on the street therefore simplification is necessary. Particular attention will also have to be paid to those who misinterpret religious scriptures and flag some of the excerpts either out of context or twist the words.

Counter radicalization has to remain alive to new trends. In the context of radicalization of youth in Europe for instance a recent Rand S tudy, "Radicalization, Linkage, and Diversity Current Trends in Terrorism in Europe," highlights that neither Al Qaeda nor Taliban carry out any substantive efforts to recruit terrorists in Europe. European Muslim youth are radicalized either individually or within a peer group by " ____radical preachers, veterans of various conflicts, webmasters of radical websites, and, more generally, charismatic "jihad entrepreneurs" act (ing) as radicalizing agents____".[5] The Study also recommends tackling terrorist networks, "between the radicalization phase and the mobilization phase," by preventing radicalization and encouraging those who have radicalized to abandon their groups. Such programmes will reduce the number of individuals embracing extremist ideology.[6]

Identifying individuals by monitoring internet chat rooms, prisons and what are known as gateway organizations such as terrorist fronts will also lead to success in tracking deviants. Interception of travel to the Af Pak area for training is also a viable means to neutralize influence of such individuals and groups. Legal tools available will have to be used effectively for this purpose.[7]

Where radicalization or threat of the same in a society is widespread, bigger programmes will have to be launched. Pakistan has recently

---

[5] Lorenzo Vidino. Radicalization, Linkage, and Diversity Current Trends in Terrorism in Europe. Rand Santa Monica. 2011. Available at http://www.rand.org/content/dam/rand/pubs/occasional_papers/2011/RAND_OP333.pdf

[6] Lorenzo Vidino. Radicalization, Linkage, and Diversity Current Trends in Terrorism in Europe. Rand Santa Monica. 2011. Available at http://www.rand.org/content/dam/rand/pubs/occasional_papers/2011/RAND_OP333.pdf

[7] Lorenzo Vidino. Radicalization, Linkage, and Diversity Current Trends in Terrorism in Europe. Rand Santa Monica. 2011. Available at http://www.rand.org/content/dam/rand/pubs/occasional_papers/2011/RAND_OP333.pdf

undertaken a counter radicalization campaign in the Swat region which may bear fruit in the future. This forms a part of the professed, "4 D strategy" of the government to include, Dialogue, Deterrence, Development and Defeating the Terrorist's Ideology and Mindset. [8] Deradicalisation obviously falls in the last named dimension. In Swat which had seen a rise in fundamentalism with a demand for implementing the Sharia, the government after enduring ignominy of violence till May 2009 launched military operations and restored order.

The campaign for political and religious moderation here has been launched by the military. The Pakistan Army has established three centres — Rastoon, Sabaoon and Feast to deradicalise juveniles, women as well as children in Swat. Given reports of child suicide bombers, the importance of deradicalisation of the young is evident. During a recent international seminar the country's Prime Minister Yusuf Raza Gillani stated, "The Swat De-radicalization Programme is, therefore, in my opinion, a model for other relevant organizations to learn from and replicate.We are aware that without an effective national strategy marked by de-radicalization, we will not succeed fully and comprehensively".[9] As of now this is work in progress and would have to be extended across the board rather than only in the Swat area. But this is welcome beginning in a country which was radicalized by the political and military elite as a tool for survival.

Eroding AlQaeda's Appeal

One of the principal political and media tasks is to erodeAl Qaeda's brand appeal. Al Qaeda has developed an exceptional ability to influence a target group by using local differences and conflicts to advantage and weaving these in the larger vision of conflict between theWest and the Rest which it purports to lead. [10] Defeating this narrative is as important if not more as

---

[8] Concluding Remarks by the Prime Minister on National Seminar on De-radicalization. 6th July 2011. Web site of Prime Minister of Pakistan.

[9] Concluding Remarks by the Prime Minister on National Seminar on De-radicalization. 6th July 2011. Web site of Prime Minister of Pakistan.

[10] Vahid Brown. Cracks in the Foundation: Leadership Schisms in al-Qa'ida from 1989-2006. Combating Terrorism Center at West Point. West Point 2007.

neutralizing organization and leadership. United States seems to be overly focused on the latter which is resulting in Americans losing the battle for the hearts and minds particularly in Islamic countries. While President Barack Obama did commence his Presidential tenure on a strong footing reaching out to the Muslim world, this initiative has now spluttered Tangible positive movement in resolving vexatious problems such as Palestine or improving relations with Iran by reaching out as Obama had declared on taking over as President has failed to take off.

The resentment in the Muslim world on assassination of Osama Bin Laden surprised many in the West but denotes the underlying sentiment of the people. This attitude should have been evident before as well A survey by Pew Research Center's Global Attitudes Project from 21 March to 26 April 2011 before assassination of Osama reveals that US Favorability Rating is very low in a majority of Muslim countries including some moderate ones as Turkey which polled 10 percent with Pakistan doing only one notch better at 11.[11] The saving grace is that the Al Qaeda is also not viewed favourably in the Muslim World with Palestine scoring highest at 28 percent.[12] But a terrorist group does not require mass popular support and even if a quarter or less of the population sees it in favourable light it is enough to facilitate sustenance. Thus particular focus on erosion of the Al Qaeda's appeal in the Muslim world and in countries as Pakistan in particular is necessary . The overall aim should be to defuse the Al Qaeda and the Bin Laden myth by capitalizing on his death and failure of his mission[3] On the other hand an external power with socio cultural and religious variance will require far greater acceptance than 50 percent by the local population.

To be credible this exercise will have to be led not by the S tate or as largesse of aid and assistance but by moderate leaders of the Muslim community. Themes and contra trends should be used to effect. For instance

---

[11] Arab Spring Fails to Improve U.S. Image. Available at http://pewglobal.org/2011/05/17/arab-spring-fails-to-improve-us-image/2/

[12] Arab Spring Fails to Improve U.S. Image. http://pewglobal.org/2011/05/17/arab-spring-fails-to-improve-us-image/2/

[13] Vahid Brown. Cracks in the Foundation: Leadership Schisms in al-Qa'ida from 1989-2006. Combating Terrorism Center at West Point. West Point 2007.

al Qaeda believes inTakfiri Islamic ideology which states that other Muslims are apostates. This is an extremist strain followed by very few people. An anti Takfiri movement in the Islamic World led by moderate clerics may gain major support given that majority of Muslims are tolerant, secular and plural.

Exposing the gory tactics of theAl Qaeda is another theme.This proved highly successful in Iraq where theAl Qaeda in Iraq under Zarqawi ignited sectarian conflict which caused very heavy casualties to civilians leading to a bad name to the organization and eventually contributed to its downfall. Such themes should be used to advantage thereby denying even the little support that the organization has.

Use of sophisticated media including new channels such as Facebook, Twitter and Google + can be made for encouraging moderationThe United States National Counter Terrorism Strategy released in July 201 1 has highlighted the aspect of employing effective communication tools to spread the message of deradicalisation. [14] However this is best passed through local intermediaries rather than even by high ranking American leaders as the President himself to carry greater credibility.

Exploiting Peaceful Revolutions –The Arab Spring

The Al Qaeda's core philosophy of violent transformation received a surprising jolt with the emergence of serial revolutions in theArab World, its core community. The Al Qaeda narrative has been anti West and to bring about transformation violence is seen as the primary pathAl Qaeda believes that change in the Islamic World can only come about after the fall of the United States. This has been challenged by revolutions inWest Asia and is the larger message that emanates from the Arab Spring.[15] The Arab spring or street side revolutions by the disempowered middle classes in the Arab World are just the opposite ofAl Qaeda's target the lower middle class and

---

[14] US Government. National Strategy for Counter Terrorism. June 2011.

[15] Daniel Byman. Terrorism After the Revolutions. How Secular Uprisings Could Help (or Hurt) Jihadists. http://www.foreignaffairs.com/ARTICLES/67697/daniel-byman/terrorism-after-the-revolutions?page=show

poverty stricken underclass as well as indoctrinated elites. These rebels have also used non violent means an anathema to the   Al Qaeda; these differences will no doubt put the terrorist group on the other side of the political divide.

There is no doubt that the al Qaeda was surprised by the Arab Spring as protests began in Tunisia on 17 December when Mohamed Bouazizi, a Tunisian street vendor, set himself on fire and Tunisian President Zine el-Abidine Ben Ali had to go in exile. This followed resignation of Egyptian President Hosni Mubarak in mid February, yet the Group did not offer any comments except a rambling by Ayman al Zawahiri in February 201 1. [16] U.S. Secretary of State Hillary Clinton in fact remarked, "I hope they [al Qaeda's leaders] were watching on television as Egyptian young people proved them wrong,"underlining non violent change happening inWest Asia and North Africa. [17]

A quote by Osama Rushdi, a former spokesperson for al-Gama'a al-Islamiyya, one of Egypt' s important jihadist group is also relevant here, Rushdi says, "If you have freedom, al Qaeda will go away   ." [18]Evidently democracy with an Islamic overtone has traction in the Muslim   World provided it also incorporates Islamic laws and traditions. [19] Support to the Arab spring by religious scholars asAbu Basir al-Tartusi and Hamid al-Ali has added to the belief that this is the way ahead. [20] Thus the Arab Spring can be used effectively to undermine the Al Qaeda in the Arab world.

Using past differences between groups is also another pathway to undermine the al Qaeda's influence in West Asia. In Egypt emergence of Muslim Brotherhood as a major stake holder in the new order is one such opportunity as past history would reveal that the group's ideologues as Sayyid Qutb have been the inspiration for Islamist extremism. [21]

---

[16] Ibid.

[17] Ibid.

[18] Ibid.

[19] Ibid.
[20] Ibid.

[21] Ibid.

The Brotherhood and Al Qaeda however do not see eye to eye and now with Zawahiri a bitter enemy of the Brotherhood for having forsaken the path of violence at the helm there is little hope that the terrorist group will get support from the emerging power structure in Egypt in case the Muslim Brotherhood has a major say in the future administration[22] Getting the Islamic parties as Muslim Brotherhood into mainstream politics is the way ahead. The more such political organizations join the path of moderate politics as a way to power rather than violence, greater is the scope for expansion of the deradicalised base against extremism . [23]

At the same time the rise of secular , liberal leaders in the Muslim World or even less fundamentalist Islamic regimes will lead to theAl Qaeda losing much of its appeal some of which is due to people's perception that their leaders have been pandering to theWest losing pride and faith in their own religion. [24] Liberalisation of these societies may also provide space for engaging the over ground and underground workers of fundamentalist and extremist groups and wean them away from the path of violence. [25]

Where the al Qaeda will gain is however due to unrest and anarchy in some countries as terrorism thrives on disorder. This is already evident in Yemen where deposition of President Saleh has resulted in a tribal civil war with Al Qaeda increasingly attempting to take advantage of the situation[26] Emptying jails in Egypt and Libya during this period is a major challenge though many former terrorist leaders released seemed to have forsaken violence yet the unrepentant amongst them are likely to exploit new found freedom to advantage. [27]

---

[22] Daniel Byman. Terrorism After the Revolutions. How Secular Uprisings Could Help (or Hurt) Jihadists. http://www.foreignaffairs.com/ARTICLES/67697/daniel-byman/terrorism-after-the-revolutions?page=show

[23] Ibid.

[24] Ibid.

[25] Ibid.

[26] Ibid.

[27] Ibid.

Operational Strategies

Neutralising Organisational Capacity

Operational strategies are designed to neutralize organizational capability of the guerrillas. The nature and type of operations would be determined by the size of the terrorist group, their organizational expanse, number of cadres, bases, activities and so on. Smaller groups are best tackled by intelligence led policing. Such operations will involve developing detailed intelligence of a groups activities and targeting these by arrest of key leaders, destruction of infrastructure or elimination of the cadre.

This can also be applied in a limited way to larger organizations. The United States has had seminal success in neutralizing the Al Qaeda leadership and potential through intelligence led operations.[28] Even before Bin Laden, a number of key leaders were killed and the organizational potential in the Af-Pak region of Al Qaeda Central has been considerably reduced. Ilyas Kashmiri, al-Qaeda's military commander and Sheik Saeed al-Masri, al-Qaeda's No. 3 leader killed are some of the main successes though firm information of Kashmiri's death is not forthcoming so far

Intelligence can be used not only to seek information but also to split leaders and the groups, frame negotiations or wean them away from their ideology to the mainstream. Frequently cash allurements, calls from family members, prospects of a peaceful life, targeting personal weaknesses can be effectively employed to neutralize leadership and cadre potential. The internet can also be effectively used to gain information and follow key leaders by hacking into emails or mobile phones and breaking into chat rooms. New threat tracking and analytical processes are available through cyber, information and communication resources which can be exploited effectively. Such means will necessitate appropriate legal approvals to be justified in a court of lawA combination of human and technical intelligence would prove most successful.

---

[28] Vahid Brown. Cracks in the Foundation: Leadership Schisms in al-Qa'ida from 1989-2006. Combating Terrorism Center at West Point. West Point 2007.

Where organizations are large and expansive as the Taliban and are using terrorism as tactics for militancy , there is a need for establishing a strong military foot print on the ground through pivots or base for operations. The aim of such operations would be to win back, "territory ," lost to the guerrillas, reclaim the same for government while carrying out intelligence led operations against the terrorist infrastructure. Such operations will be expensive in terms of troops and will have to be supported by government will, people support and well trained and motivated armed forces. The Afghanistan counter insurgency model is an ideal contemporary example of this paradigm.

The difference between counter terrorism and counter insurgency would be evident in terms of the expanse of influence of rebel groups, wider support of the people that they enjoy in the latter and necessity for deploying military forces in what is popularly known as a security grid. On the other hand counter terrorism operations can be conducted by deploying intelligence bases and information networks and surgical strikes, physical or by drones. The bane in such a model remains that of collateral damage which the guerrillas tend to exploit by trapping security forces in operations that lead to large number of civilian deaths. This will also be the case when indirect fire power of air, attack helicopter or artillery and missiles is used where lack of adequate information may lead to loss of innocent lives.

To obviate the backlash of civilian anger , military deployment are invariably accompanied by development as well as civic actions to create a facilitating environment for troops to operate by winning over hearts and minds of the local population. There is also a need for a cultural connection to be established, thus foreign forces in an alien land may always be at a disadvantage howsoever well meaning their efforts are.

Decapacitation of the leadership as a strategy has received much attention after the assassination of Osama Bin Laden. The unique nature of operations with high capability enjoyed by the United States in intelligence and operational sphere need to be underlined which may not necessarily the be case for other nations before investing resources in this sphere. On the other hand covert and clandestine operations offer a unique opportunity for targeting leadership which has been used by many countries in the past. This does remain a principal though perhaps not the most important component of a counter terrorism strategy.

Apart from physical elimination a number of other tactics can be used to de-capacitate a leader, including arrest and reconciliation. Isolation is another tactic which has been successfully employed by the United States against the Al Qaeda leadership thereby considerably reducing their potential to control their groups and contain the spread. Thus Bin Laden and Zawahiri were virtually driven into obscurity for many years and even though they were able to communicate through couriers their potential were considerably reduced.

For targeting support structures such as financial networks, arms and drug running links, intelligence will again be the primary tool to be employed by deploying a vast network on the ground and addressing each facet separately. International cooperation and regulatory mechanisms such as Financial Action Task Force (F ATF)[29] an inter -governmental body for promotion of national and international policies to combat money laundering and terrorist financing could be employed effectively for capacity building. These measures have to be supported by strong legal and judicial mechanisms. Similarly international cooperation against drugs and criminal syndicates supporting terrorism is called for. Future operational strategies will also have to include gaining information and intelligence of Nuclear, Biological, Chemical and Radiological terrorism and countering threats from the same.

An all encompassing national and international judicial framework will have to support counter terrorism. Presently the United Nations is the largest and most significant coordinating organization which provides international authority to target terrorist groups and leaders. The sanctions regime was first established by resolution 1267 (1999) on 15 October 1999. This regime has been modified and strengthened from time to time by subsequent

---

[29] Details of the F ATF can be obtained at their website http://www.fatf-gafi.org/pages/0,2987,en_32250379_32235720_1_1_1_1_1,00.html

resolutions, 1333 (2000), 1390 (2002), 1455 (2003), 1526 (2004), 1617 (2005), 1735 (2006), 1822 (2008), 1904 (2009) and resolution 1989 (201 1). The names of targeted individuals and entities are on what is known as the Al-Qaida Sanctions List.[30]

The Security Council obliges all States to, "freeze without delay the funds and other financial assets or economic resources, including funds derived from property owned or controlled directly or indirectly; prevent the entry into or the transit through their territories; prevent the direct or indirect supply, sale, or transfer of arms and related material, including military and paramilitary equipment, technical advice, assistance or training related to military activities, with regard to the individuals, groups, undertakings and entities placed on theAl-Qaida Sanctions List". 234 individuals [14 individuals related to Taliban were removed in July 2011] and 89 groups and undertakings have been included as of July 2011 on this list.[31]

Countries publish their own list with related stipulations such as the United States Foreign Terrorist Organisations list or the Indian Unlawful Activities (Prevention)Act, 1967 which has banned a number of organizations designated as terrorist. These Acts oblige a state entity to take action against such organizations and restrict legal transactions with them thereby performing the function of containment and deterrence.

While a number of operational strategies have been specified herein, these are a bouquet of capabilities which a country or a force may employ based on circumstances and best effects that can be obtained on the ground. The guiding principle remains that of minimum essential force to achieve optimal results, something that will have to be identified by counter terrorism leaders. The people and political leadership's willingness to accept loss is another determinant. An ideal combination can be achieved only through experience.

---

[30] http://www.un.org/sc/committees/1267/

[31] List and other details are available at http://www.un.org/sc/committees/1267/aq_sanctions_list.shtml

Internal Security or Homeland Security Strategy

Introduction

Given all pervasiveness of terrorist targets, the basic principle of counter terrorism will be to protect people and assets from violence. Even as the guerrillas are neutralised on the ground, in case they are able to continue to inflict pain by launching attacks, success for counter terrorist forces will be elusive. Thus there is a need for establishing a strong internal security grid which protects almost every citizen and critical asset. For this purpose each country will evolve its own model based on local circumstances, constitutional and legal provisions. Two models are outlined here for information, Homeland Security of the United States and Internal Security as it is more popularly known in India. The role, mission and outline components of each model is provided as per succeeding paragraphs with only brief comments at the end for it is envisaged that success is as much dependent on right tasking as in effective implementation.

US Department of Homeland Security (DHS)

The role of DHS is to ensure a safe, secure and resilient US homeland particularly against terrorism and other hazards.[32] There are five missions as follows:-

1. Prevent terrorism and enhance security.

2. Secure and manage borders.

3. Enforce and administer immigration laws.

4. Safeguard and secure cyberspace.

5. Ensure resilience to disasters.

The core concept of homeland security is inter agency coordination between federal, state and local governments, law enforcement, the private

---

[32] The US Homeland Security Model is based on details provided at http://www.dhs.gov accessed on 20 May 2011.

sector, international allies, and individual citizens, communities, and organizations and improve awareness of risks and threats, working to build safer and more resilient communities and develop innovative approaches and solutions through advanced science and technology

The various components and operative agencies of the DHS are as follows:-

(a) The Directorate for National Protection and Programs works to advance the risk-reduction mission.

(b) The Directorate for Science andTechnology is the primary research and development arm.

(c) The Office of Policy is the primary policy formulation and coordination component.

(d) The Office of Health Affairs coordinates all medical activities to ensure appropriate preparation for and response to incidents having medical significance.

(e) The Office of Intelligence and Analysis is responsible for using information and intelligence from multiple sources to identify and assess current and future threats to the United States.

(f) The Office of Operations Coordination and Planning is responsible for monitoring the security of the United States on a daily basis and coordinating activities within the Department and with governors, Homeland Security Advisors, law enforcement partners, and critical infrastructure operators in all 50 states and more than 50 major urban areas nationwide.

(g) The Domestic Nuclear Detection Office works to enhance nuclear detection efforts of federal, state, territorial, tribal, and local governments, and the private sector and to ensure a coordinated response to such threats.

(h) The Transportation Security Administration (TSA) protects the nation's transportation systems to ensure freedom of movement for people and commerce.

(i) United States Customs and Border Protection (CBP) have a priority mission of keeping terrorists and their weapons out of the U.S.

(j) United States Citizenship and Immigration Services grants immigration and citizenship benefits, promoting awareness and understanding of citizenship, and ensuring the integrity of the immigration system.

(k) United States Immigration and Customs Enforcement (ICE), promotes homeland security and public safety through the criminal and civil enforcement of federal laws governing border control, customs, trade, and immigration.

(l) The United States Coast Guard is one of the five armed forces of the United States and the only military organization within the Department of Homeland Security. The Coast Guard protects the maritime economy and environment, defends maritime borders, and saves those in peril.

(m) The Federal Emer gency Management Agency (FEMA) builds, sustains, and improves capability to prepare for , protect against, respond to, recover from, and mitigate all hazards.

(n) The United States Secret Service (USSS) safeguards the nation's financial infrastructure and payment systems to preserve the integrity of the economy and protects national leaders, visiting heads of state and government, designated sites, and National Special Security Events.

Indian Internal Security Model

The Ministry of HomeAffairs (MHA) is the central ministry and equivalent of the DHS responsible for internal security in India. [33] It has multifarious responsibilities not restricted to homeland security comprising of centre state relations and administration of UnionTerritories amongst others. The MHA

---

[33] The Indian Ministry of Home Affairs model is based on details provided at http:// www.mha.nic.in/ accessed on 21 May 2011.

is not directly responsible for public order and policing which are the responsibilities of the State government. However some functions related to internal security of the MHA are as follows:-

(a) Overall policy and coordination of internal security to include counter insurgency and terrorism.

(b) Management of para-military forces.

(c) Border management

(d) Disaster management.

(e) Monitoring the situation, issuing appropriate advisories, provide manpower and financial support, guidance and expertise to the State Governments for maintenance of security peace and harmony without encroaching upon the constitutional rights of the States.

The various components of the MHA specifically dealing with internal security issues highlighted above are as follows:-

(a) Department of Border Management, dealing with management of borders, including coastal borders.

(b) Department of Internal Security, dealing with police, law and order and rehabilitation.

(c) Department of Jammu & Kashmir (J&K)Affairs, dealing with the constitutional provisions in respect of the State of Jammu & Kashmir and all other matters relating to the State excluding those with which the Ministry of External Affairs is concerned.

(d) Disaster Management Division responsible for response, relief and preparedness for natural calamities and man-made disasters (except drought and epidemics). The Division is also responsible for legislation, policy, capacity building, prevention, mitigation and long term rehabilitation.

(e) Foreigners Division deals with all matters relating to visa, immigration, citizenship, overseas citizenship of India, acceptance of foreign contribution and hospitality

(f) Human Rights Division deals with matters relating to the Protection of Human RightsAct and also matters relating to national integration and communal harmony andAyodhya.

(g) Internal Security Division, which comprises of two sub divisions as follows;-

(a). Internal Security-I Division deals with matters relating to internal security and law & order, including anti-national and subversive activities of various groups/extremist organizations, policy and operational issues on terrorism, security clearances, monitoring of ISI activities and Home Secretary-level talks with Pakistan on terrorism and drug trafficking as a part of the composite dialogue process.

(b). Internal Security-II Division deals with arms and explosives, narcotics and Narcotics Control Bureau (NCB), National Security Act.

(h) Naxal [Left Wing Extremism] Management Division monitors the Naxal situation and counter-measures being taken by the affected States with the objective of improving ground-level policing and development response as per the location specific action plans formulated/to be formulated by the affected States, and review with the concerned Ministries/Departments to ensure optimum utilisation of funds released under, and proper implementation of various developmental schemes in the Naxal affected areas.

(i) North East Division deals with the internal security and law & order situation in North-Eastern States, including matters relating to insurgency and talks with various extremist groups operating in that region.

(j) Police Modernisation Division handles all items of work relating to modernization of State Police Forces, provisioning/ procurement of various items for modernization of Central Police Forces, police reforms and police mission. It also deals with the security of VIPs/ vital installations/religious shrines/places except Ram Janam Bhumi/ Babri Masjid, Ayodhya.

(k) Policy Planning Division deals with matters relating to policy formulation in respect of internal security issues, international cooperation on counter-terrorism, international covenants, bilateral assistance treaties and related items of work.

Some of the key organizations under the Ministry of Home Affairs which contribute to internal security are as follows:-

(a) Counter Terrorism and VIP Protection. National Security Guards (NSG).

(b) Central Paramilitary Forces. Assam Rifles, Border Security Force – Border management and counter insurgency and terrorism.

(c) Central Police Organisations to include Central Reserve Police Force, Central Industrial Security Force – Law and order, counter terrorism and industrial as well as transportation security.

(d) National Disaster Management Authority (NDMA) – Disaster management

(e) National Intelligence Grid (NA TGRID) under process of establishment – Intelligence and surveillance of critical data bases.

(f) National Investigation Agency (NIA) – Proactive and after action investigation of terrorism and insurgency related incidents.

(g) Central Bureau of Investigation – Criminal investigations and financial fraud.

(h) Intelligence Bureau – Internal intelligence.

(i) Bureau of Police Research and Development. Research and development on internal security and counter terrorism.

Given the responsibility of law and order and terrorism at the State level, local police are also organized to meet this challenge and are the first responders are it in terms of information and intelligence, reactions and investigations.

Comparison Responsibility

United States Homeland Security	India's Internal Security Management
Counter Terrorism	Internal Security including counter militancy and counter terrorism - Provision of support to State governments.
Border Security	Border Management
Preparedness, Response and Recovery	Disaster management
Immigration	Immigration and Customs
Cyber security	Responsibility is with Ministry of Communications and Information Technology
Nil	Narcotics Control

Comparision of Structures

United States Homeland Security	India's Internal Security Management
Customs and Border Protection (CBP)	Border Security Force and Customs
Federal Emergency Management Agency (FEMA)	National Disaster Management Agency (NDMA)
Transportation Security Administration (TSA), Aviation Security	Bureau of Aviation Security (BCAS)
U.S. Citizenship and Immigration Services (USCIS)	Immigration and Customs
U.S. Coast Guard	Coastal Police. Coast Guard operates under the Ministry of Defence.
U.S. Secret Service	Intelligence Bureau for internal intelligence only, external intelligence agency operates under the National Security Adviser
Information Sharing, State and Major Urban Area Fusion Centers	Multi Agency Centre, State and District Multi Agency Centre. NATGRID or National Intelligence Grid is being established
Secure Identification	UIAD Unique Identity Programme
National Terrorism Advisory System	Not Available. National Counter Terrorism Centre (NCTC) is in conceptual stage
Protected Critical Infrastructure Information (PCII) Program	Not Available, responsibility for critical infrastructure security is that of concerned agency with provision of Central Industrial Security Force by the Ministry of Home Affairs.
Nil	Narcotics Control Bureau (NCB)

As would be seen the type of mechanisms put into place are based on unique constitutional, legal and governance mechanisms of each country. Effective functioning of these is important so that they can deliver timely results. A debilitation in operations invariably shows up through repeated terrorist attacks as in the case of Mumbai, India's commercial capital which has been the subject of terror strikes over a period from 1993 to 201 1. To that extent United States Homeland Security model is more effective than Indian internal security asAmerica has succeeded in avoiding a major terrorist attack after 9/11. The splitting of responsibility between the Centre and the State in India also militates against accountability . Synergy in various organizations and their coordinated functioning is also important particularly of information and intelligence. For this purpose Information Technology can be used to some effect but the main challenge is that of overcoming turf wars, resistance to sharing and bureaucratic inertia. Thus all aspects in this sphere from organizational design to effectiveness deserve attention.

Strategies to Counter State Support: Case Study South Asia

General

The importance of SouthAsia in the overall global counter terrorism matrix is evident with the United S tates National Counter Terrorism S trategy released in July 2011 devoting a full section to, "SouthAsia: Al-Qa'ida and its Affiliates and Adherents".[34] The base of operations of the Al Qaeda has been identified in this Document in Pakistans Federally Administered Tribal Areas (FATA) radiating threats to the, "U.S. Homeland and interests as well as to Pakistan, Afghanistan, India, Europe, and so on".[35]

Another major characteristic of this region is lack of multi lateral or bilateral cooperative security structures and mechanisms. Where these exist they have failed to yield positive resultsA National Bureau ofAsian Research Special Report 21 of December 2009 on, "CounterTerrorism Cooperation in South Asia: History and Prospects," by Sumit Ganguly , a noted scholar

---

[34] US Government. National Str ategy for Counter T errorism. June 2011.

[35] Ibid.

on SouthAsia reiterates the point that counter terrorism cooperation in South Asia has been limited and states have been prone to use terrorist groups as proxies to serve their foreign policy and security interests.[36] Sumit Ganguly feels that organizational weaknesses of states in South Asia are such that even if they were to decide to cooperate they do not have requisite human or capital resources in terms of forensic laboratories, intelligence or coercive capabilities to implement cooperation.

There are however some notable instances of counter terrorism cooperation in South Asia, the first is between India and Sri Lanka which saw India deploy the Indian Peace Keeping Force (IPKF) in the country in the wake of the Indo Sri Lanka Accord of 1987. This period however remained short lived as a change in political regime in Colombo led to pull out of IPKF even as changes happened in the political spectrum in New Delhi with the Prime Minister who initiated intervention Mr Rajiv Gandhi making way for Mr V P Singh. India however returned to support Sri Lanka in containing the spread of L TTE by choking of f supply routes to the organization from 2007 onwards which finally led to decimation of the guerrillas by the Sri LankaArmy in May 2009.

Another noteworthy cooperation which has worked is that between India and Bhutan, wherein the Royal Bhutan Government launched offensive raids on camps of the United Liberation Front ofAssam (ULFA) within its own territory in 2003 in an operation known as All Clear. This operation resulted in considerable losses to the ULFA including some of its key leaders, though the outfit continued to sustain operations in the State.. An offshoot of the same stream of cooperation against the ULFA is positive approach of the Sheikh Haseena government in Bangladesh when it came to power in December 2008. Haseena ordered withdrawal of support to all groups operating in India's North East from Bangladeshi soil.A number of leaders were handed over to Indian intelligence agencies in covert operations. This led to considerable losses to the main North East groups including the ULFA, National Democratic Front of Boroland (NDFB), the United National

[36] Sumit Ganguly. *Counter Terrorism Cooperation in S outh Asia: History and Pr ospects.* National Bureau of Asian Research. Washington. December 2009.

Liberation Front (UNLF) which operates in Manipur and National Liberation Front of Tripura (NLFT). The approach by the Awami League government indicates positive inclination for cooperation which also included reining in the intelligence agency Director General of Forces Intelligence (DGFI). The DGFI a bi product of ISI had the same reputation of supporting dissidence in India as a policy.

Of late Shanghai Cooperation Organisation (SCO) comprising of China, Russia, Kazakhstan, Kyr gyzstan, Tajikistan and Uzbekistan as members with countries as India, Pakistan and Iran as observers is actively considering cooperation on counter terrorism and drug trafficking amongst other issues. This was particularly evident after the killing of Osama Bin Laden. "The recent elimination of terrorist No. 1 Osama bin Laden is beyond all doubt a success of the United States, but it is in no way a victory over international terrorism," Kazakh Foreign Minister Yerzgan Kazykhanov told a meeting with his counterparts from SCO states in June 201. "Craving for revenge, the supporters of al Qaeda, the Taliban movement and other terrorist and extremist organisations may cause a new wave of terror as they attempt to avenge for the death of their leader," he added.

There is also particular concern in SCO over the situation in Afghanistan after the departure of the United States in 2014. Thus Kazykhanov said, "In our view, the situation in Afghanistan will keep tension high in the region, remaining a source of terror, extremism and illegal trafficking of drugs and weapons." SCO is thus a bridge between South and Central Asia and how it will contribute to counter terrorism is unclear but is likely to be a new initiative if it takes off.

Three countries in South Asia will be at the forefront of counter terrorism, Pakistan, Afghanistan and India. Strategies related to these are outlined as per succeeding paragraphs.

Strategy - Post Bin Laden - Pakistan

Pakistan's response to the assassination of Bin Laden on its territory has created concerns of its contribution to counter terrorism in the region. There has also been intensification of terrorist violence in the country which was already on the edge. "The situation in Pakistan, throughout Pakistan since Osama bin Laden's death, has seen an intensification of fighting and an intensification of violence," said Pascal Cuttat, the International Committee of the Red Cross's head in Pakistan in July 201. "Not the least also because violence is increasingly reaching the big towns — Peshawar and Karachi both have seen sharp increase of violence," he said. "For the immediate future, we expect more of what we see now ," added Cuttat.

The killing of bin Laden has also generated greater suspicions against foreigners, who are now finding it harder to work in the country . "It has made the work considerably more difficult," said Cuttat, pointing to increased hurdles for permits to work in Pakistan. "There is throughout Pakistan today considerably higher suspicion with regards to any foreigner working in the country," he added.

The challenge with reference to Pakistan is to persuade the government, army and the people to accept that terrorism is the main security threat to the nation. Neutralizing non state actors of varying hues, extremist, separatist and sectarian is essential for which a comprehensive approach led by the civilian leadership is necessary Building institutional capacity is also important and cooperation with state actors will be the way ahead for peace and stability. The army and the ISI will also have to abandon terrorism as a strategic tool for fostering instability in India and Afghanistan. This will require a fundamental shift in the overall state policies and strategic thinking which have been embedded over a period. Thus the approach will have to be not just to build internal capacity but induce the state to change its national strategy to dismantle the infrastructure of terrorism and fundamentalism contained there in.

In line with this approach, United States National Counter Terrorism Strategy 2011 proposes to induce Pakistan to sustain pressure on the terrorist groups, "leadership structure, command and control, organizational capabilities, support networks, and infrastructure__," and is willing for , "_____greater Pakistani-U.S. strategic cooperation across a broader range of political, military, and economic pursuits will be necessary to achieve the defeat of al-Qa'ida in Pakistan andAfghanistan". Apart from theAl Qaeda and Taliban, the Lashkar-e Tayyiba (LT) has also been flagged in the United States National Counter Terrorism Strategy 2011 as it is seen to have the ability to not just carry out terrorist attacks in South   Asia but also affect regional stability and escalate tensions between India and Pakistan.   [37] Implementation of this intent into tangible action by Pakistan is however a key challenge as is evident from a discussion of aid and drone attacks, two complimentary but diametrically different strategies adopted by the US in Pakistan with perhaps the same indifferent results.

Economic aid is a standard tool used to seek greater cooperation of a country. United S tates has committed considerable economic and development resources to induce Pakistan to build capacity and undertake counter terrorism operations. This includes civilian and military aid and is linked to tangible measures by Islamabad. There are provisions to cut off aid and the administration is required to certify each year that Pakistan is complying with conditions laid down in Bills such as Kerry-Lugar-Berman under which the Congress has provided funds. C Christine Fair   , noted Pakistan specialist with extensive grounding in the region has however observed that economic and military assistance to Pakistan has not so far resulted in a change in approach and castigates the US government for being lenient towards Islamabad. She cites how Secretary of State Hillary Clinton certified on March 18 that Pakistan was in conformity with all the security stipulations of the Kerry-Lugar-Berman bill for providing civilian and military when it was not fully compliant[38]

Fair also finds it, "Pretty shocking," that this assertion was made by the State Department even as the Pentagon was preparing for a raid on Bin Laden on 18 March and the Secretary of State was well aware of the possibility of the guerrilla leader well entrenched in Abbottabad.[39] Possibly Hillary Clinton may not have wanted to reveal that something was cooking

---

[37] US Government. National Str ategy for Counter T errorism. June 2011.

[38] Graham Webster .After bin Laden, Still No Choice for U.S. with Pakistan. An Interview C. Christine Fair May 26, 2011. National Bureau of Asian R esearch Washington. 2011.

[39] Graham Webster .After bin Laden, Still No Choice for U.S. with Pakistan. An Interview C. Christine Fair May 26, 2011. National Bureau of Asian R esearch Washington. 2011.

on this front but then it always had the option of exercising a waiver on national security grounds rather than giving a blanket sanction.

There is some debate however if development aid is a panacea to dissuade terrorism. A recent article in ForeignAffairs by a group ofAmerican writers including Fair has questioned this premise with reference to Pakistan.[40] The writers argue that the rationale that terrorism takes roots only amongst the poor is faulty as there is no evidence to show that economic aid will change the attitude of people away from terrofThey cite that United States and its allies have already directed billions of dollars in development assistance to Pakistan and   Afghanistan in the last ten years, with no demonstrable impact on the spread of Islamic militancy.[41]

The authors substantiate their hypothesis by a survey of rural Pakistan which measured attitudes toward four main militant groups: al Qaeda; the Afghan Taliban; Lashkar-e-Taiba, Jaish-e-Mohammed, Hizbul Mujahideen operating in Jammu and Kashmir; and sectarian groups such as Lashkar-e-Jhangvi and Sipah-e-Sahaba. The survey indicated that support in rural and urban poor in Pakistan to militant groups is much lesser than the middle class as the former suffer the most in the event of a terrorist attack.   [42] However the authors' argument that this should lead to reduction of development aid and assistance may be flawed given that overall penury and unemployment does draw youth towards terrorism.

A parallel case is that of unilateral drone attacks by the US in tribal areas of Pakistan. As per noted author and counter terrorism analyst Peter Bergen, "On average, only one out of every seven U.S. drone attacks in Pakistan kills a militant leader". More over drone attacks have neither resulted

---

[40] Graeme Blair, C. Christine F air, Neil Malhotr a, Jacob N. Shapiro. Pakistan's Middle Class Extremists. Available at http://www.foreignaffairs.com/articles/67976/graeme-blair-c-christine-fair-neil-malhotra-jacob-n-shapiro/pakistans-middle-class-extremists

[41] Graeme Blair, C. Christine F air, Neil Malhotr a, Jacob N. Shapiro. Pakistan's Middle Class Extremists. Available at http://www.foreignaffairs.com/articles/67976/graeme-blair-c-christine-fair-neil-malhotra-jacob-n-shapiro/pakistans-middle-class-extremists

[42] Graeme Blair, C. Christine F air, Neil Malhotr a, Jacob N. Shapiro. Pakistan's Middle Class Extremists. Available at http://www.foreignaffairs.com/articles/67976/graeme-blair-c-christine-fair-neil-malhotra-jacob-n-shapiro/pakistans-middle-class-extremists

in reduction of terrorism inAfghanistan and Pakistan on the other hand the number of incidents has gone up says Bergen. This has also not acted as a deterrent for those from outside the region and particularly the   West to travel to Af Pak region for training. 150American and European youth had been reported to have gone to the tribal areas for training in 2011.[43]

Bergen recommends that drone strikes should be undertaken in cooperation with Pakistan which is also a demand by Pakistani leadership. This will lead to greater transparency which can be enhanced by releasing footage of strikes regularly . Thus Bergen recommends that, "A more transparent drone-strike program, with greater overt cooperation from Pakistan, would increase accountability , in particular regarding civilian casualties. It would also help lessen the fervent anti-Americanism in Pakistan by demonstrating that the war against militants in the tribal regions is in the interests of both Pakistan and the United States". [44]

The above instances highlight the key challenge of getting Pakistan fully on board the international counter terrorism campaign. As per Fair, Pakistan urgently needs a "big idea" that will help restructure the way it understands its security threats and potential role in the regionWithout this, Pakistan will continue menacing the region.[45] What ever be the case pursuing Pakistan to deradicalise, to reconsider terrorism as a tool of state policy to decouple from terrorist groups and non state actors and to cooperate with the international community will remain a key policy objective for the international and regional community led by the United States and India and supported by China and Russia. How this equation works out remains to be seen.

---

[43] Peter Bergen and Katherine Tiedemann. Washington's Phantom War. Available at http://www.foreignaffairs.com/articles/67939/peter-bergen-and-katherine-tiedemann/washingtons-phantom-war

[44] Peter Bergen and Katherine Tiedemann. Washington's Phantom War. Available at http://www.foreignaffairs.com/articles/67939/peter-bergen-and-katherine-tiedemann/washingtons-phantom-war

[45] Graham Webster .After bin Laden, Still No Choice for U.S. with Pakistan. An Interview C. Christine Fair May 26, 2011. National Bureau of Asian R esearch Washington. 2011.

Afghanistan: Sustained Support

United States National Counter Terrorism Strategy 2011 outlines approach in Afghanistan as to, "weaken the Taliban, bolster the Afghan Government, and strengthen the capacity of Afghan military and civilian institutions to secure the populace and effectively govern the country ____." [46] Despite this Afghanistan will remain a key concern as International Security Assistance Force (ISAF) spearheaded by North Atlantic Treaty Organisation (NATO) with a major contribution by the United States has started reducing the profile in the country in 2011.

Given current indications, a weak Afghanistan on the edge of failure is a worst case scenario or in the vortex of internal and regional power conflicts is the best case one in 2014. In all likelihood, power contests, internal and external in Afghanistan are likely to continue beyond 2014. The identity of players may change from NATO to regional to include Russia, China, Iran, Pakistan, Central Asian Republics and India with the United States continuing to retain presence in the region. It would be therefore appropriate to evolve a strategy that can face up to these challenges in the years ahead. Some considerations in the evolving situation are flagged herein

Given likely tensions between Pakistan and Afghanistan, the role of regional organizations as the Shanghai Cooperation Organisation (SCO) if it gains prominence or bilateral and multilateral relations between traditional partners as India, Russia and Iran with new ones in Central Asia as Kazakhstan and Kyrgyzstan can prevent a covert or overt conflict. Balancing with the United States will also be essential as it will continue to occupy an important position despite plans to disengage from Afghanistan in 2011. The likelihood of US bases in Afghanistan would be another point of contention both within the country and more so regionally

Afghanistan's power structure is likely to represent a triad, the central government in Kabul, regional heads in the North or South who may retain a high degree of autonomy and Taliban which may or may not merge with

---

[46] US Government. National Strategy for Counter Terrorism. June 2011.

the former. Creating a cooperative or at least a non confrontational arrangement between these forces will be important which may boil down to active operations against those elements who continue to resort to violence while bringing as many groups who want to join the mainstream into the political system. The international community will have to establish clear red lines with Islamabad from the very outset to ensure that pre 9/11 situation is not obtained in the country and it does not support anti government forces such as the Haqqani network.

Afghanistan will also require extensive economic aid and assistance. A stable Afghanistan will in turn see economic expansion be it in primary sectors as mining with the Hajirak mines offering good prospects, developing industrial infrastructure or transportation linkages. Steel plating or hard wiring critical facilities and personnel will assume importance as the security grid may be diffused once ISAF leaves. While the Afghan National Army and Police are evolving rapidly there will be elements suspect to subversion, thus providing higher levels of security will be necessary. In a worse case scenario, a UN mandated force will prove a good asset for stability in Afghanistan in the near future.

India: Building Capacity

India's counter terrorism challenges are two fold, transnational terrorism and capacity building. India is facing cross border terrorism from Pakistan in Jammu and Kashmir in particular and the country at large with support provided to various groups including the most dangerous Lashkar Taiyyaba. This has led the country to believe that this is a form of war called as proxy war in the Doctrine for Sub Conventional Operations by the Indian Army. Proxy war has been defined as "a war conducted between nations utilising non state players to fight on their behalf. In any case, at least one of them must employ a third party to fight on his behalf. The extent and type of support provided by the States involved in proxy war will vary but financial and logistical support are normally always provided". [47] Of late there has been a shift in approach and while relations had particularly deteriorated

---

[47] Doctrine for Sub Conventional Operations. Army Training Command. Shimla. 2004.

after Mumbai 26/1 1, some improvement is seen with Indian leadership exercising restraint in naming Pakistan in serial bomb attack again in Mumbai on 13 July 2011. A comprehensive dialogue has commenced but is likely to be held hostage to another major terrorist attack in the country what ever be its origins.

Internal capacity building is another key challenge for India as it remains vulnerable to terrorist attacks despite efforts to improve capacity. Security sector reforms in India are in the first phase which follows the cycle of conception, debate, dissemination, acceptance and execution. These are also undertaken episodically particularly after an incident of terror . Thus after the complex terrorist attack in Mumbai on 26 November 2008, known as 26/11 a number of reforms were proposed.Those that followed accepted philosophy such as enhancing first responder effectiveness or strengthening multi agency centres have been implemented. Others as National Intelligence Grid (NATGRID) or National Counter Terrorism Centre (NCTC) are languishing because these are in the debate and dissemination stage even though the government has already gone in for implementation. It is therefore unlikely that progress will be smooth or speedy

There is also resistance as NATGRID is feared to lead to disclosure of individual transactions. Apart from privacy there are genuine concerns of use of such data for political purposes.These fears cannot be wished away given legacy of use of agencies for collection of political intelligence as much as for operational or criminal. The bureaucratic challenge of resistance to sharing is another grey area which will have to be tackled.

Living in what India' s Home Minister Mr P Chidambaram has characterized as, "troubled neighbourhood," India is facing formidable diplomatic and capacity building challenges which if not taken care of early may lead to slow down in growth and trashing of the dream of an emerging economic power.

Conclusions on CounterTerrorism Cooperation

Regional cooperation is known to succeed when common security architecture is in place. In South Asia despite challenges of transnational terrorism no such arrangement exists and given major differences between States in the region bilateral cooperation has not been successful. South Asia Association for Regional Cooperation (SAARC) charter proscribes discussion on bilateral and contentious issues, thus counter terrorism cooperation cannot be discussed therein. The SAARC Convention on Suppression of Terrorism in 1987 only caters for anti hijacking but the same was not used to effect when an Indian Airlines plane was hijacked enroute from Kathmandu to Delhi to Kandahar in December 1999.

Working towards cooperative counter terrorism architecture is thus necessary for South Asia. The first step could be a joint counter terrorism centre for research and training. Bangladesh in fact had come up with just such a proposal but did not receive support from other SAARC countries and thus has not been pursued thereafter .[48] For all this to happen Sumit Ganguly feels that the push will have to come from outside the region, that is either by the United States or Europe.

In operative terms, bilateral cooperation invariably fails when one state perceives the other using terrorism as a state policy against its legitimate interests including infringement of territorial sovereignty as Pakistan in Jammu and Kashmir or when a state is perceived as acting in its sole interests rather than in a mutually beneficial relationship as Sri Lanka felt when it asked the IPKF to leave.

When two political parties with opposing ideologies and world views with traditional hostility are in power again there is limited scope for bilateral cooperation which is evident from the example of Bangladesh wherein cooperation between Bangladesh and India is low when Bangladesh Nationalist Party (BNP) is in power as opposed to the Awami League.

To summarise the discussion so far, cooperation on counter terrorism between states seems to be working best when the following conditions are met:-

---

[48] Sumit Ganguly, *Counter Terrorism Cooperation in S outh Asia: History and Pr ospects.* National Bureau of Asian Research. Washington. December 2009.

- **Mutual National Interest** . When states see actions against terrorist groups to be in mutual interest the scope for cooperation is high.

- **Political congruence**. Where two political parties having favorable inclination towards each other are in power in neighbouring countries there is hope for greater cooperation. On the other hand when a military dictator is in power scope seems to be reduced due to two factors lack of legitimacy of the regime and propensity of the uniform to sustain conflict in self interest

- **Control of security and particularly intelligence establishment by the civil government** . An important facet is who actually controls the military and intelligence establishment in the country. Civilian control does lead to better cooperation.

- **Intelligence cooperation**. Sharing of information and intelligence seems the ultimate form which results in targeting non state actors and adversarial terrorist groups and should be strived for.

Conclusion

Benchmarking strategies distilled in this Chapter to achieve the Bottled Genie Scenario of containment of Al Qaeda in particular and terrorism in general would possibly reinforce the argument. For this a comparison is carried out with United States National Counter Terrorism Strategy July 2011. The goals outlined in the US Strategy fall broadly in strategies proposed for countering terrorism which have been hyphenated alongside :-

- Protect the American People, Homeland, and American Interests – Internal Security Strategy.

- Disrupt, Degrade, Dismantle, and Defeat al-Qaeda and Its Affiliates and Adherents – Operational Strategy.

- Prevent Terrorist Development, Acquisition, and Use of Weapons of Mass Destruction - Operational Strategy.

- Eliminate Safe havens - Operational and Countering State Support to Terrorism Strategy.

- Build Enduring Counterterrorism Partnerships and Capabilities – Cooperation and Unity of Effort outlined as principles.

- Degrade Links between al-Qaeda and its Affiliates and Adherents - Operational and Political Strategy.

- Counter al-Qaeda Ideology and Its Resonance and Diminish the Specific Drivers of Violence that al-Qaeda Exploits – Political Strategy.

- Deprive Terrorists of their Enabling Means - Operational Strategy.[49]

---

[49] US Government. National Str ategy for Counter T errorism. June 2011.

Index

Symbols

160th Special Operations Aviation Regiment (SOAR) 40

A

Abbottabad
2, 3, 9, 27, 29, 30, 31, 32, 33, 34, 36, 40, 44, 46, 55, 89, 91, 92, 93, 94, 99, 111, 121, 131, 175

Abimael Guzman 14

Abu Basir al-Tartusi 157

Afghan Peace and Reintegration Plan 150

Al Qaeda
1, 2, 3, 6, 7, 9, 10, 13, 14, 16, 18, 19, 20, 21, 23, 28, 30, 32, 33, 42, 43, 45, 49, 52, 53, 54, 55, 57, 58, 60, 61, 62, 64, 65, 66, 67, 68, 69, 70, 71, 72, 73, 74, 75, 76, 77, 78, 79, 80, 81, 82, 83, 84, 85, 87, 89, 90, 91, 94, 95, 99, 101, 104, 105, 106, 107, 109, 111, 112, 113, 114, 115, 116, 117, 118, 119, 120, 122, 124, 125, 127, 129, 130, 131, 133, 135, 136, 141, 142, 145, 146, 148, 152, 153, 154, 155, 156, 157, 158, 159, 161, 171, 174, 182

Ideology, Narrative and Population Support 124

Leadership 126

Organisation 127

State Support to Terrorism 129

Support Structure 128

al Qaeda
1, 2, 4, 6, 7, 9, 20, 25, 27, 28, 29, 30, 43, 48, 52, 53, 54, 55, 56, 57, 58, 59, 61, 63, 65, 66, 67, 68, 69, 70, 71, 72, 73, 74, 75, 77, 78, 79, 80, 81, 82, 84, 85, 87, 91, 103, 105, 110, 112, 121, 122, 123, 124, 125, 126, 127, 128, 131, 141, 142, 147, 156, 157, 158, 173, 176

Al Qaeda - The Base 66

Adaptive Network 71

Al Qaeda Central 77

Al Qaeda in the Arabian Peninsula 79

Nasir al Wahishi 79

AQIM 80

Abu Musab Abdel Wadoud 80

Organisation 66

Zawahiri Era 73

Al Qaeda Beyond Bin Laden 57

Al Qaeda in India 113

Al Qaeda In South Asia 112

al Shabaab 83

al-Gama'a al-Islamiyya 157

Assad al-Jihad 9

Assam Rifles 168

Audrey Kurth Cronin 10

Ayman al Zawahiri 3

S

T

U

W

www.ingramcontent.com/pod-product-compliance
Lightning Source LLC
Chambersburg PA
CBHW060839100426

42814CB00016B/423/J